PEOPLE PROCESSES

PEOPLE PROCESSES

HOW YOUR PEOPLE CAN BE YOUR ORGANIZATION'S COMPETITIVE ADVANTAGE

RHAMY ALEJEAL

This book is presented solely for educational and entertainment purposes. The author and publisher are not offering it as legal, accounting, or other professional services advice. While best efforts have been used in preparing this book, the author and publisher make no representations or warranties of any kind and assume no liabilities of any kind with respect to the accuracy or completeness of the contents and specifically disclaim any implied warranties of merchantability or fitness of use for a particular purpose. Neither the author nor the publisher shall be held liable or responsible to any person or entity with respect to any loss or incidental or consequential damages caused, or alleged to have been caused, directly or indirectly, by the information or programs contained herein. No warranty may be created or extended by sales representatives or written sales materials. Every company is different and the advice and strategies contained herein may not be suitable for your situation. You should seek the services of a competent professional before beginning any improvement program. The story and its characters and entities are fictional. Any likeness to actual persons, either living or dead, is strictly coincidental.

PEOPLE PROCESSES

How Your People Can Be Your Organization's
Competitive Advantage

ISBN   978-1-5445-1178-8 *Hardcover*

       978-1-5445-1177-1 *Paperback*

       978-1-5445-1176-4 *Ebook*

LIONCREST
PUBLISHING

This book is dedicated to my wife, Elizabeth—my inspiration, motivation, and love. And also to my amazing family, David, Kathy, Amanda, Emily, and Ryan, who provide a rock-solid foundation of support for my life.

CONTENTS

INTRODUCTION

Getting hired to be the executive director of a nonprofit and working for a cause you care about sounds like a dream job, right? For many, it is. Christy was a forty-something manager who was looking for just an opportunity. Finally, she got it. Still, immediately after she found her dream job, she knew she had a problem.

The sixty-year-old nonprofit that hired her was a staple of its small Tennessee community, providing books and educational materials for children. While its mission was robust, Christy soon found out its HR and staffing processes were a stagnant mess. Of their approximately fifty employees, many had been in their roles for decades and were resistant to change. The previous executive director, for example, had held the title for twenty years. The person before him? Thirty years. All the top positions were filled, and turnover was extremely low. Partly because of this, the organization wasn't growing and couldn't retain smart, young, fresh talent. There was no room for advancement.

Not only had the hiring and retaining practices not changed in decades, but neither had day-to-day business operations. Because of the antiquity of the business, Christy found that everyone from associates to the C-suite had stacks of rote, repetitive tasks—literally, stacks of stupid paper. A tired old system was sucking the life out of the organization.

TAKING CHARGE TO INSPIRE

Christy wasn't having any of this. She was a dynamic, aggressive executive director who truly believed in the mission of the organization. She didn't want to spend her time approving payroll; she wanted to make a difference in a community that desperately needed the organization to expand its services to meet people's needs.

So she did.

After six months with Christy at the helm, the nonprofit had an increased revenue of 15 percent while reducing overhead by 10 percent. Legacy community partnerships deepened, and new ones formed. Some high-level executives chose to leave the company rather than change their ways, and their positions were quickly filled by talented new team members. The efficiency of those positions changed too. In fact, across the company, management was now spending only four to five hours completing routine tasks that used to take up to thirty-six hours per week—a change that allowed team members across all departments to focus more on how to move the organization forward rather than just keep it afloat.

Christy accomplished this goal by taking advantage of technology to streamline operations and implemented systems that freed her staff to do rewarding work again. Upper management stopped being paper pushers and became idea people who could create and execute lasting change in the organization, and Christy led the charge.

At the crux of Christy's strategy was a unified HR system, a technology that allowed the team to have an accessible location that facilitated every function related to each employee, from payroll to compliance and everything in between. For the employees, the system was convenient and simple. It led to higher morale and strengthened training practices. For Christy and the rest of her executive team, the HR system removed the rote, repetitive tasks of managing people and instead made room for the inspiring, change-inducing tasks of influencing and leading people.

THE STATE OF HR TODAY

Christy's story is one of success, but many organizations and businesses are still dealing with stagnation as a result of tired, cumbersome HR tasks—or, worse, no systems at all!

Maybe you're the CEO of an organization who has been outgrowing your company for years. As you look back, you begin to see the issues that have fallen through the cracks that keep popping up internally. Maybe you realize that, like Christy's team, your employees are struggling to wade through outdated systems and that this burden is dragging down morale. If this describes your organization, it's likely you view HR as a necessary evil or just an afterthought. It's also likely you've invested significantly in human capital by hiring employees within your organization without truly investing in a system to properly onboard, manage, and engage staff. The result? Unmotivated employees, unchanged processes, and expensive turnover.

In many cases, the HR conundrum is a result of mis-aligned priorities.

Consider, for example, the amount of time and resources your company invests in client acquisition and product/service delivery. Now, compare that to the amount of time and resources you invest in onboarding, training, and retaining employees. If the discrepancy between the two is large, you likely have an HR problem.

There are myriad other signs that something needs to change in your organization. If an unhappy client leaves, alarm bells are set off throughout management. "What did we do wrong? What did we promise that we didn't deliver? Where did we fall short? Why was our competition able to steal them away from us?"

However, when an employee leaves, alarm bells rarely sound, and questions are rarely posed. Many managers simply chalk up the loss to a flaw with that employee, a bad fit, or a symptom of their particular industry.

The truth is, if you want to deliver on the promises you make to your clients, your people are the vehicle by which you follow through on those commitments. Your people are the backbone of your business. If you're struggling to motivate them and not batting an eye when they leave, you're missing something.

This disconnect in HR often occurs because management spends a large percentage of its time on repetitive tasks and paperwork instead of on the company's people and its mission. Outdated systems have such a high labor requirement that all too many business leaders, from CEOs to CFOs to HR managers, spend way too much time reviewing paperwork and signing off on employee requests. Executives and managers in this situation often feel like their plates are too full to take on anything extra.

Their "time investment" in "HR" is already huge, so they can't imagine doing more work on this costly time sink called HR that seems to just drag the organization down. They are spending too much time bailing out the boat and not enough time steering the ship. Leaders bogged down with routine tasks are too busy working *in* the organization rather than *on* it—and that's a problem.

Luckily, I've got a solution.

SHIFTING THE FOCUS TO PEOPLE

My wife and I started Poplar Financial, a company that provides HR solutions to help businesses simplify and streamline their HR processes. In nine years' time, we've helped hundreds of businesses across the United States understand and find solutions for the growing pains that accompany the HR side of conducting business in today's marketplace.

When we started our company, we were a product provider helping our clients navigate the worlds of payroll and benefits, such as insurance coverage and paid time off. We soon realized we needed to expand our services to truly accelerate our clients' businesses, so we shifted our business model. We became a provider of comprehensive, tailored HR and employee benefits services, but that's not all. Besides designing and implementing processes by which employees receive their payroll and benefits, we also find ways to ensure they appreciate and understand their benefits too.

In other words, our primary goal is to help our clients make HR about people again. We help our clients—whether they're nonprofits, private businesses, small cities, or other entities—retain top talent by communicating their value via their systems and employee benefits.

At Poplar Financial, we provide personalized HR products to help businesses remain focused and moving forward. This work is the crux of what we do every day, and for good reason. I understand my clients because, at one point in time, I was just like them. I focused solely on our software—making it sexy, making it sell, making sure it solved problems—and it did. We doubled in size four years in a row. In the midst of all this growth, however, I still felt worried and unsure. Could my team handle the boom in growth? Could I scale up my labor system without it imploding? Would the talented people I hired be on their game, every day, enough to get this all done?

After I shifted my focus back to my people—through a process I'll explain in the following pages—my doubts evaporated, my teams' performance improved, and our growth exploded even more.

In the past, I would lie in bed at night worried about staffing. Where would I find the right people? Would they stay? How much should I pay them? How much time would they need to learn our processes?

Today, my system works. I'm confident in it, and so are my clients. I work with companies that could now take on ten new Fortune 1000 clients and bring in qualified team members who not only fit the required talent and skill levels but who could be fully trained in their functional roles in as little as two months. *That's* scale, and that's what we offer our clients.

LEVERAGING THOSE YOU LEAD

Are you a CEO, executive director, HR manager, or other leader struggling with antiquated HR systems, high turnover, or other stagnation in your organization? If so, it's time to turn your focus inward and examine your people processes to ensure they're working for you.

In the following pages, you'll find a roadmap for navigating, systemizing, and—this is key—automating your HR processes so you can remove the daily drudge work and get back to the business of actually leading. Then, you can focus on growing, training, and mentoring those you lead—your people—into your true competitive advantage.

This process works because when you properly develop and manage your people, you'll find you have more confidence acquiring, servicing, and maintaining clients; accomplishing your organizational mission; and delivering on your promises to your team and your customers.

I understand this may sound like a lofty goal, and that's because it is. However, my entire business is built on making the complicated uncomplicated, so you can bet I have a system.

WHAT CAN YOU EXPECT FROM THIS BOOK?

This book presents my system in three parts:

Part 1. In Chapters 1 through 4, we'll take a deep dive into the employee life-cycle events (onboarding, offboarding, annual review work, and ad hoc events) in both traditional and modernized organizations. We'll discuss how these systems interact in an effective system and how they're handled in ineffective systems. After reading Part 1, you'll have an understanding of what employee life-cycle events could look like for your organization and how that modern experience translates into a more efficient and more motivated employee base.

Part 2. In Chapters 5 through 11, we'll explore HR system components in both traditional and modernized organizations. System components include staples such as onboarding; benefits and compensation; timekeeping, accruals, and scheduling; payroll; reporting systems; compliance systems; and cultural communication. We'll discuss in detail how making each of these components better through automation can improve the overall system.

Part 3. In Chapters 12 through 16, we'll discuss concrete tools and strategies you need to implement positive change in your organization. In short, you'll find a road-map to your success! These aren't the only chapters filled with action, though. Throughout the book, you'll find direction to online resources and supplemental tools, including a weekly podcast, checklists, and download-ables to help your organization refine and leverage its people processes and gain a competitive advantage.

Let's get started!

If you are ready and committed to changing your people processes, do me a favor. Email me directly at rhamy@ poplarfinancial.com with "I'm committed to better people processes" in the subject line. I won't spam you, and I won't try to sell you anything, but take a minute to actually perform an action—to *do* something so you know this is going to actually help revitalize your organization.

PART ONE

THE LIFE CYCLE OF YOUR MOST IMPORTANT BUSINESS ASSET

ONBOARDING

AN IMPORTANT WELCOME

Onboarding, at its most basic, is the ritual of gathering and auditing new employee information. But it should be so much more. Beyond a job application, you also need to know a new employee's withholding status, emergency contacts, current mailing address, phone number, and other information. If your organization provides a uniform, you'll also collect clothing and shoe sizes. Similarly, if your organization caters meals, you might also gather a new employee's dietary requirements during the onboarding process.

Besides gathering initial data, onboarding is also your opportunity to introduce your company's mission, culture, and values to your new hire. This step is not to be overlooked; in fact, outside of gathering basic information, the number one purpose of onboarding should be to acclimate your new employee to your company's *why* and engage them so they remain excited to work for you.

After you've collected initial data and communicated your company's mission, the next step in the onboarding process is to train your new hire on HR systems, policies, and benefits. For example, you'll teach your employee how to clock in and out, access the company intraweb and databases, navigate secure areas of the organization (if applicable), and more. You'll also explain benefits and compensation, outline management and personnel practices, and show your employee how to request time off. It's imperative to spend time communicating the benefits you offer thoroughly so your employee is not only familiar with their compensation package, but they appreciate it holistically—a key distinction that can be easy to overlook.

Once you've gotten the personal data you need; signed the necessary legal documents; communicated the HR systems, benefits, and compensation information; and ensured the employee understands the mission of your organization, it's time to transition the employee to the supervisor-led work for which they were hired. Those are the nuts and bolts of onboarding, but it's rarely a seamless process and, done poorly, can negatively affect your employee and your organization. Let's explore.

CASE STUDY: TAMARA'S ONBOARDING

In the promising and frenetic months leading up to Tamara's college graduation, she researched jobs online and applied to many of them. At a local job fair, she found a private college with an open marketing executive position well suited to her skills and education. She enjoyed meeting the people, interviewed for the role, and got a job offer. She was so excited that she told all her friends, and she prepared to start in two weeks. Prior to her first day, Tamara learned everything she could about the college by reading online. It was a small, growing institution with about forty people in her department, and she saw potential to move up the ranks.

Tamara arrived to her first day of work with a spring in her step, and the manager greeted her at the door. They toured the campus, and Tamara was soon introduced to a cubicle desk with a giant stack of paperwork. She filled out her W-4 and I-9, and she completed her direct deposit information. An HR associate gave her a thick booklet of information about employee benefits for which she'd be eligible in ninety days, and she was also given paperwork about the organization's retirement program. Tamara was also asked to complete a nondisclosure memo. After thirty minutes of trudging through the stream of paperwork, Tamara began quickly scanning pages and signing at the bottom with no real understanding of the details. She brought all the papers back to the HR associate, where she then received a security card, a user name, and a password to clock in and out. Tamara went out to lunch with a new coworker and then went right back into the paper storm.

Her manager was supposed to introduce Tamara to the team and train her, but due to her busy schedule, she couldn't start until Wednesday. So Tamara spent all of Monday and Tuesday performing tasks that didn't truly apply to her work. On Wednesday, things were rushed, and Tamara was already two days behind. Her timekeeping duties were covered in a rushed manner, among other things, leaving her with a lot of questions. To Tamara, the onboarding process that could have been welcoming left her feeling overwhelmed, disconnected, and confused about her place in her new organization. Nevertheless, she decided to just go with the flow. She decided to just ask her new coworker, Chad, about any specifics she needed to know as they came up, as he seemed really friendly and helpful.

ONBOARDING PITFALLS

Tamara's story is not uncommon. In many organizations, much of the information a new hire needs is communicated in a disjointed, tribal manner. Many new employees are hesitant to ask questions and, if you haven't built a rapport with them, are unsure to whom to direct those questions—an orientation issue that can lead to confusion.

For example, a supervisor in the marketing department might answer the same question differently than a manager from accounting. When this occurs, it's difficult to create a unified experience. Handing a new hire like Tamara a stack of paper and expecting her to learn and digest it on her own isn't a warm welcome or an efficient use of time.

Imagine if a new client of your organization had the same onboarding experience as Tamara. Maybe your company has spent months and thousands of dollars attracting the business. Then, the client sends a check, and you send them eight hundred pages of detritus that does little to communicate your company culture or commitment to that client. You then say, "Go forth and read. Fill everything out, sign the legal document, and let us know if you have any questions."

Onboarding doesn't work that way with a client, and it shouldn't work that way with an employee either, but it does, far too often. Many times, once a new hire is finally finished completing the paperwork, they go to work with substantial knowledge gaps that will constantly pull them back when it's most urgent. Two months later, when Tamara wants to take a three-day vacation or is sick, for example, she won't know how to handle it. Likely, she'll call her friend Chad directly and ask what the procedure is to request time off. This takes both Chad's and Tamara's time, and it leads to inconsistent processes among departments. It also interrupts the important work they should be doing to further the organization's goals. Ultimately, these knowledge gaps set the employee and the company up for cascading failure from both a resource and a personnel perspective.

When onboarding isn't done well, there are knowledge gaps on the HR side too. For example, Coleen is the director of HR at the college where Tamara recently started working. She didn't know Tamara was hired until three days before payday because all of Tamara's paperwork had gone to a different supervisor's desk untouched. At the last minute, Coleen received an email reminding her to pay the new employee. Caught completely off guard, she called her supervisor and had to start from scratch. To make matters worse, Tamara worked the first two weeks without clocking in and out, as that system wasn't properly communicated to her. In this situation, all Coleen understands is that Tamara was hired for a specific job title and will receive a specific pay, but her knowledge stops there. The two have not met, so they have not established trust. HR is just a department where paperwork goes to die, from Tamara's perspective.

Tamara and Coleen's situation—and many others like it— effectively relegate HR to an accounting office, creating a ripple effect: HR feels like a transactional department rather than a resource that helps your company and your employees.

If you think such a snafu is uncommon, think again. In my early years in the field, I was shocked at the number of times companies' HR departments didn't know someone was hired. Or worse, sometimes HR is the only office that can *do* the hiring at all, and those departments are consistently overwhelmed. They regularly hire people for positions unrelated to HR, and they don't necessarily hire the right people matched to the right supervisor. In this example, even if Coleen had learned about Tamara in a reasonable time frame, there would still be the issue of processing a giant stack of paper and all the back and forth accompanying it—in other words, a giant waste of time.

THE HR BLUES

Many HR processes are time sensitive, and delays and missing information can cause more than simply logistical issues. Consider this scenario: an HR associate picks up a new employee's information sheet and tries to enter the information into the retirement portal—its own animal and where all employee retirement accounts are created and maintained. The HR associate is given the new hire's hourly rate, but he does not know how many hours she worked or is expected to work. In addition, the employee was hired for a part-time position, but the HR associate is unsure whether that is for twenty hours a week, and thus eligible for the 401(k), or for five hours, and therefore ineligible. He continues to input the data he has, leaving gaps along the way. When he begins to input her information into the payroll and benefits system, the associate realizes the employee included her children's names and their dates of birth but not their social security numbers.

Now the HR associate must go back to the employee or her supervisor to gather the additional information. It's been a few days since the paperwork was sent in that HR took to get around to reviewing it. This back and forth can take a few days—the culmination of an arduous process that ultimately delays the arrival of the new employee's insurance cards. At this juncture, the employee is upset because she doesn't have insurance and hasn't had it for two weeks. HR is stressed, attempting to rush and account for errors made during data entry. The scenario is time consuming and, most importantly, sends a message that HR is a time sink—a necessary evil that should be avoided if at all possible.

Another common scenario is one in which an employee has been working for an organization for several weeks but, due to the workload over in HR, the employee hasn't received sexual harassment training—a large issue in today's world— and the company mission and values were overlooked during onboarding. There was a statement in the handbook covering their mission, but to say it was "glanced over" is overestimating the time spent on it. HR knows they are supposed to send the employee through trainings on situations like these, but so much time has lapsed that an HR associate decides to simply ask the employee if she has any questions about the sexual harassment policy. More often than not, the employee will not have questions, and it's easy for the HR associate to move on and mark that box on the form as complete. By now, the employee has the impression that these required trainings are unimportant, that "it's just paperwork." That this uninformative, boring paperwork is what HR does—an attitude that will come back to haunt HR and the employee in the end.

The bottom line is clear: every interaction your employee has with the company influences whether they love or hate their job and your organization. Compare it to your first meeting with a potential client, the first orientation at a new school, or the first time you meet someone new—all times to put in effort, ensuring the experiences are memorable and positive.

WHAT SHOULD ONBOARDING LOOK LIKE?

Onboarding shouldn't be a dreadful experience for you or the new employee. Instead, it should be a way for you to welcome someone to your team and leave them feeling motivated and happy to be there. The process itself, as with every HR procedure, should be automated, repeatable, compliant, and scalable. To accomplish this effectively, you should be involved *before* the employee actually comes on board, preferably via a recruiting platform through which you can manage the process more effectively. At the least, your HR department should be present from the time the employee receives the offer or welcome letter forward. Managing onboarding effectively goes beyond creating good vibes between the employee and your company; it should move the new hire as quickly as possible to substantive job training and work, expediting integration into the company so they can contribute.

TAMARA'S BEST DAY

Here's how Tamara's onboarding experience should have gone. Tamara received not only a job offer from the private college, but she also got a letter in the mail and a follow-up phone call from her new manager. She can't wait to start work; in fact, her excitement level is likely the highest it will ever be working with the organization.

Tamara doesn't start her new role for two weeks, but HR sent her login information so she could access the HR platform ahead of time. From there, Tamara electronically completed preliminary documents and performed basic tasks, such as verifying her address and withholding information. She filled out her direct deposit information, W-4, handbook receipt, noncompete agreement, and more.

Next, resources within the platform helped begin Tamara's orientation into the organization. She learned about the company mission and culture, and she watched short introduction videos from the CEO, HR manager, and other departmental managers.

After Tamara completed orientation and received an in-depth introduction to company culture, she was prompted to delve into details about benefits—not through stacks of paper but via modules or videos in the platform. She learned about the amazing benefits, like maternity leave, sabbaticals, 401(k) matching, retirement planning, wellness programs, life insurance, disability, paid time off (PTO), and more. The communications were designed to help Tamara understand all the benefits and, through that understanding, increase her appreciation for her new job.

With benefits background in hand, Tamara moved on to learning about various HR systems, such as how to clock in and out, request vacation, and more. She was introduced to their overall project management system, and got a good grounding in what she would actually be doing most days.*

---

* Note: These processes for "early training" change depending on your state and the type of employee you are hiring. It's important, in all states, that this early training be voluntary. It's also important that if they do not do it themselves before hire, they have the opportunity to do it on their first day. Either way, by systematizing this process and making it attractive and accessible, you will accomplish your goal. Do not make it mandatory to do prior to hire, as that can lead to wage and hour violations for unpaid work.

On Tamara's first day of work, she felt comfortable and knew faces, not just names and job titles. She also felt prepared, as she'd thoroughly reviewed policies and had already received training on basic HR systems within the organization. Her first activity at her new job was a thirty-minute call or meeting with the HR director to get to know one another. Because the hard work was already done, the "paperwork" was automatically processed and sent to vendors, synced with payroll, and updated in timekeeping automatically. The HR director took the time to let Tamara know he was available and there to help. The purpose of the meeting was purely to establish the relationship, answer questions, and help Tamara feel comfortable coming to HR with any problems she may have. From there, Tamara spent the rest of her day acclimating to company culture. She was introduced to the rest of the team, shadowed employees, and went to lunch with her new coworkers. The next day, she moved into the task-specific training for which she was hired. No paperwork needed, no back and forth for missing or incorrect info, no "just signing it" even though she didn't really read it.

On top of all this, all the info she went through during onboarding is still available to her in her HR portal. If she needs to review it or has questions—bam! It's easy for her to get to the same place she manages her profile info, requests time off, or researches her benefits.

AN OUNCE OF PREVENTION

Significant time, labor, and investment is required to front-load an onboarding system with the modern automation and communication tools that exponentially improved Tamara's experience. When I paint the above picture for many HR leaders, their response is something like, "There is no way I could set something like that up. Look how busy I am. I just don't have the time!" Fair enough. My answer in return is, "It sounds like you don't have the time not to." Once it's in place, you have a scalable environment that sparks an employee's love of the organization, heads off a stream of questions down the road, and creates an environment where employees know they can come to you for additional help. Your HR team need only input basic information from the application, if that, and the system automates the rest. You don't have the time for anything more than that if you are going to actually act as a force multiplier for your labor force and if you actually want your people to be your organization's competitive advantage.

The key to the success of modern HR environments is simple: an ounce of prevention is worth a pound of cure. Because the "people processes" are efficient and auto-mated, you get to spend your time on prevention, and you can focus on developing employees and improving the system itself. You can initiate more videos, better information, different programs, and more robust train-ing, which will drive the organization forward and avoid issues later. Ultimately, a well-designed and executed onboarding process means less work for your HR team, not more.

Some may believe that leveraging technologies—i.e., automation—detracts from the human aspect of the workplace, but experience has shown that the opposite is true. Technology is helping to clear the way for a return to the human aspect of HR. As an organization, your people are your biggest investment, and everyone is served by shifting the focus from rote, routine work to improving the human experience, starting from day one.

GO DEEPER

To grab an onboarding checklist to get you started, visit **PeopleProcesses.com**. Click **Resources**, then **Onboarding Checklist**.

ANNUAL REVIEW WORK

TIME FOR REFLECTION AND PROGRESS

Tamara had a wonderful first year at her job. She took on new responsibilities, adjusted well to the culture, and excelled on several projects for which she took ownership. One day, her supervisor stopped by her desk to remind her that her anniversary was coming up. He said he'd like to talk to her about her performance over the year and handed her documents to fill out, instructing her to review her own performance. The documents included standard prompts and asked her to rate her performance, identify what she could do to improve, and note her future goals.

The next week, Tamara sat down with her supervisor for a quick meeting to discuss the form. He reviewed the document, agreed with her goals, promised to help her achieve them, and provided feedback about what she could work on to be a better fit for the organization. At the close of the review, he mentioned that because it was Tamara's work anniversary, she would receive a 5 percent raise. Overall, Tamara felt satisfied with the review, although she found it stressful to fill out the paperwork over which she'd been judged. She also did not have a real understanding of what she did to earn, or not earn, a bigger raise. She wasn't sure what next year really held for her, her position, or her income.

When benefits renewal approached two months later, Tamara learned her benefits were going to change in January. Before her raise, Tamara made $38,000 annually. After her raise, she made $39,900 annually. However, at this point, she learned the new benefits plan would cost $150 more per month for her and her spouse and included a $1,000 increase in her insurance deductible. She realized that, given the increased cost of benefits, she wasn't making any more money than before, despite her self-perceived and actual exceptional performance in the workplace.

WHY TYPICAL ANNUAL REVIEWS FALL SHORT

Tamara's experience is an example of a poor performance review system for several reasons. First, she viewed the required paperwork as something she'd be judged on, so she answered the prompts as positively as possible. In the end, it was essentially a repeat of her original interview, and both Tamara and her supervisor felt a level of superficiality about the exchange. Second, the performance review did not include information about the change in benefits—a factor that essentially negated her raise.

Although Tamara's performance review could have been better, it's important to note that only a small percentage of organizations conduct them at all.

In organizations that do conduct annual reviews, they're often not even as systemized as Tamara's was. In these situations, performance reviews are often conducted on an ad hoc basis and are based more on tenure than merit. Although some supervisors may excel at recognizing performance and pushing to get an employee a raise, if there isn't an organization-wide process, those efforts can feel scattered and may not be fruitful. Some managers push for raises, and others don't. Of those who push, some get them and others don't. All in all, it leads to frustration among both the managers and employees who try to justify their positions to the organization. In bad cases, it can and does lead to employees losing motivation. After all, if no one really notices when they slack off—and, in the end, they are not rewarded for performing above the norm—why try? If Larry over there got the same raise as you even though you worked twice as hard as him and single-handedly secured a giant account, why put yourself through all that work?

Whether an organization conducts a formal annual review or not, one fact remains: during any given year, an employee will have at least two annual events—their anniversary (and its possible raise) and benefits renewal. In the majority of organizations, these are entirely separate events, even though both are integrally linked—not just by the fact that they happen once a year but also because they revolve around the employee's compensation for their work.

WHAT'S IN IT FOR ME?

When conducted poorly, annual reviews offer few upsides for the employee, HR, or the company. For the employee, the review is stress-laden with paperwork and often completed with vague information that provides little actionable information. For your HR team and the organization as a whole, the review is often completed solely to have a backup in the event you need to justify termination or a raise. During the standard review process, questions are vague (such as, "How would you rate your performance?"), employers rarely ask about the employee's view of the company, and therefore, they get little to no feedback about the organization and structure.

Performance reviews should, in fact, be an opportunity

for the employee to provide feedback about your company and vice versa—a dynamic I estimate fewer than 10 percent of organizations embrace. This hesitance is understandable, as good reviews can take on an element of fear from the perspective of both parties. By making it a two-way street, both the employer and employee take it more seriously, and the likelihood of actual useful information being exchanged is increased dramatically.

Now, you may be afraid to engage in a conversation about your employee's view of the company to avoid having to remedy a situation, or you may fear your employee will leave for another opportunity if your weaknesses as an organization are put on display. Such fear of awakening unrest is common for smaller companies. I realized this myself as a small business owner, and I have seen it with many of my clients who have thirty to fifty employees. I understand it can seem easier to skip the review altogether or sidestep asking difficult questions that may expose weaknesses in your business, but doing so leaves a trail of missed opportunities.

THE ANNUAL REVIEW BIG FIVE

When performance reviews are superficial and don't serve a purpose other than checking some compliance box, it is completely reasonable that managers, employees, and business owners just phone it in or skip it entirely. Why even do it at all? What is the actual purpose that performance reviews should accomplish?

EMPLOYEE PERFORMANCE

From an HR perspective, the purpose of the employee performance portion of a review is to identify *what you don't know*. It should not be a critique for the employee or a conduit to expose their faults. Performance reviews should focus on uncovering information previously unnoticed in your analysis of the person. You already know whether they show up on time and perform their duties well. Instead of asking basic questions, ask some of the following:

- What did you do this year that we don't know about?
- What did you do this year that you think was your best work?
- Is there anything you did this year that you feel lacked in performance, and what was the reason? Is there any information you can give us to shed light on those specific situations?

EMPLOYEE SATISFACTION

Employee satisfaction is the biggest component most performance reviews omit. Gauging this factor is critical in terms of your ability to make decisions about the future of the employee in your organization. It's one of the best things you can learn about from an annual review. To address your fears, your employee is no less likely to leave if explicitly asked about satisfaction in the workplace. Instead of asking your employee how she likes her job, for example, ask her the following:

- What parts of your job do you like most?
- How do you feel you're treated in relation to others with the same role at this organization?
- How do you feel you're treated in relation to others who do the same job at other organizations?
- Do you feel under- or over-utilized?
- Do you have enough time and resources to complete your tasks?
- Do you feel as though your work here truly shows your skills and allows you to excel? If not, how can we remedy that?
- Do you feel like we treat our employees and clients well?
- Do you feel like your supervisor supports you and does their job well?

The goal of asking these questions is to gather actionable information. In order to accomplish this effectively, there must be an element of trust between your HR team and the employee—a feat accomplished by viewing and treating your people as a competitive advantage. If you establish a solid relationship between your HR team and your employees outside of the traditional paperwork and transactional mentality, you have turned your HR department into a place that can inform company strategy and decision-making—a move that ultimately explodes the value of the company.

BENEFITS AND COMPENSATION

After you've gathered information about your employee's perceived performance and overall satisfaction, you can combine it with your observations to form a decision about compensation. For example, you may decide to give a pay raise or bonus. Keep in mind benefit changes are normally separate from a work anniversary and are often visited on a calendar-year basis—a dynamic that can make it difficult for you and your employee to gather a holistic view of the compensation package.

For example, say that an employee receives a raise after his annual review. Then, in October, management announces the organization has seen triple-digit growth and thus will be granting each employee a $5,000 bonus. When benefits renewal comes around a few months later, that same employee will either get a pay cut or a pay raise, depending on the benefits available to him. All three events—an annual bonus, an annual pay raise on an anniversary, and an annual cut or rise in take-home pay and coverage at benefits renewal—touch the same imperative: an employee's pay. Calendar-based plans such as this one almost guarantee compensation is not wholly tied to employee performance, which can leave managers and employees alike confused and frustrated.

A better approach is to tie compensation, benefits, and performance together and keep the anniversary separate. For example, say you hire a new employee in November. December is when open enrollment occurs for your January 1 renewal, so that employee should go through the performance review process two months after hire. The same should happen the following December. Their anniversary is a wonderful day to give them a pat on the back or an encouraging note, but it should have very little to do with their compensation.

Approaching benefits and compensation in this way allows you to be transparent when costs go awry. For example, if your insurance costs are going up 20 percent, you'll be able to notify your employees that the company is now spending significantly more on each person's benefits package. If your company plans to offload those costs to your employees, many of them will have just gotten a virtual pay cut—something you can then take into account when you do your performance review. If you want to keep that employee—and remain competitive in the market—

you can adjust his pay accordingly at that time and avoid the timeline confusion.

TRAINING PROCESSES AND UPDATES

Annual review work is necessary, but it can also slow workflow because it amounts to a mountain of meetings and administrative tasks. Take advantage of this semi-downtime by pushing out training across your organization. Update HR systems, address compliance opportunities, offer refresher courses on basics like phone etiquette and customer service, or fine-tune implementation programs.

Many of these additional interactions can be accomplished via automated means, so they won't require a great deal of employee or employer time. Regardless of your delivery method, though, it's both opportunistic and necessary to utilize annual review time to address problem areas and grow as an organization.

GOAL SETTING

While you are soliciting feedback from employees and giving reviews, it's time to set and communicate organizational goals for next year. You must understand your goals as an organization in order to accurately address bonuses, promotions, strategic vision, and position needs. Delivering this information during the performance review provides clarity, leadership, and direction—all components an organization needs to succeed.

There are many potential scenarios around goal setting as an organization, and not all are good. For example, your company could be losing money, shrinking, or experiencing slow growth. In these situations, it's your job as an HR professional or business owner to communicate where the company is now, where you want it to be next year, and how the employees can help along the way.

Some may argue it's best to forego transparency in negative scenarios like these, but I disagree. Your employees are not oblivious to what is going on in your organization, so it's best to control the message. Tell your team the truth, and then tell them the plan moving forward. This approach will help your employees see how their work contributes to the growth of the organization and, ultimately, how they'll be rewarded financially for being a part of that growth.

If your company is expanding and profiting like mad, transparency is still the path forward. Failing to explain organizational goals can cause just as much employee resentment when a company doubles in size. Yes, an employee may receive a 5 percent pay raise, but they still won't know what the future of the company looks like for them. In this situation, you may tell your employee that the company intends to double in size again next year but that it can only happen if the organization hits a specific set of benchmarks. Then, you have the opportunity to explain what that employee can do to help reach those benchmarks for her department—and, if successful, what that will mean for her position and compensation.

AUTOMATION'S ROLE IN THE REVIEW PROCESS

Automating everyday chores goes a long way in the review process. When data collection, scheduling, and other time-consuming tasks are done for you, you're able to spend time making positive changes in your organization.

In a modernized people process setting, all you have to do as an HR manager is read performance reviews, then help your organization implement feedback to improve the health of your organization and the lives of your employees. It frees you up to focus on the why of your annual review process and the information exchanged instead of the laborious rote work of actually getting these things completed—that's what automation offers.

Here is a glimpse at key tasks related to the review process that can be automated or streamlined using technology:

- Notifying employees of upcoming performance reviews
- Notifying managers of upcoming performance reviews they need to conduct
- Soliciting and compiling feedback about company performance
- Communicating the strategic plan of both the overall organization and individual departments
- Sharing changes in benefits packages, such as those that affect insurance premiums and retirement plans
- Gathering employee election changes and sending them straight to payroll for automatic implementation
- And much more!

GO DEEPER

I'll discuss automation in-depth in Part 2. Performance reviews can be overwhelming if you have never done them before. If you need some help getting started, go to **PeopleProcesses.com**. Click **Resources**, then **Intro Performance Review Checklist** to download a simple checklist that covers the basics of performance reviews.

AD HOC DUTIES

HR IMPERATIVES

Aside from joining the company, leaving the company, or having been with the company for a full year, there are specific ad hoc duties—that is, events you can't schedule but can plan for—that trigger HR actions. By addressing these with forethought, you can reduce the time and resources expended by your HR staff and actually turn these duties into opportunities that make your employees love working at your organization. Let's explore some common examples, note how they're often handled in non-modernized organizations, and discuss how to improve these experiences for you and your employees.

PROMOTIONS, PAY RAISES, AND CHANGES IN JOB DUTIES

Not all ad hoc events are negative; in fact, many aren't—

starting with promotions, pay raises, and changes in job duties. While these are all positive outcomes likely brought on by excellent job performance, your HR team can dampen their luster if you fail to handle them effectively.

PITFALLS IN A NON-MODERNIZED ORGANIZATION

Pay raises or changes in duty can come out of the blue and are often not adequately addressed by HR—an unfortunate situation that can leave employees with more questions than answers.

One of my friends, Jeff, worked for an organization for years and was given one week's notice that he was being promoted to a new position. Understandably, he was excited. Although nobody from management or HR discussed pay with him, he assumed the promotion would come with a raise. He had worked for this organization some time and was looking forward to learning new things, improving his department, and making his mark on the company.

Unfortunately, his movement into management, while ultimately successful, was painfully complicated, time-consuming, and energy sapping. You see, upon promotion to management, my friend was required to complete multiple manager "trainings" during his first month in the new role.

Not just any training, either—the worst kind. Each week, corporate HR taught a class for the first two hours of a Tuesday, in person. My friend would drive two hours to arrive at HQ at 7:00 a.m. Then he and his colleagues would get a paper packet, watch a video, have a question-and-answer session during which no one asked questions, and take a paper test. While these trainings checked all the boxes in a compliance sense, Jeff was 90 percent mentally checked out the whole time. He was thinking about what he needed to do later and was frustrated at his time being wasted. After all that, he would drive two hours back to his normal location in order to start his day at 10:00, so he consistently felt behind.

Drive two hours, wage and hour compliance, drive two hours. Drive two hours, bullying in the workforce, drive two hours. Drive two hours, cybersecurity, drive two hours. Drive two hours, sexual harassment, drive two hours. Drive two hours...

On and on. For three months. Thirteen Tuesdays!

In addition to the poor training, Jeff was also disappointed when he got his first paycheck in his new role and noted no change. After sharing his concerns with his new boss, he learned his salary increase had been submitted, and they weren't sure why his pay was not changed. Through back and forth with HR and his new boss, they got it straightened out (with back pay)—a full two payrolls later.

After the payroll change went through, he learned that the promotion also included a change to his benefits. Now, he would be eligible for participation in their major medical insurance. He heard this news from another new manager who had gotten a packet on the benefits from his boss. Jeff then had to go and chase HR again for information on his new benefits, for which he eventually got the paperwork. Unfortunately, due to the delay, he had only one day left to make his benefits decision, and he didn't know whether this new insurance was better than his wife's plan on which he was currently covered. In the end, he decided to just leave it alone until next year when he would hopefully have adequate time to review his options.

I know Jeff's story sounds like a series of one-off mistakes and terrible luck, and that's true. It took a series of bad systems and choices in order to turn what should have been a great experience into one that sucked morale out of Jeff, killed nearly all of his enthusiasm for his new role, and made him consider whether all the extra work of his promotion was even worth it. The systems in Jeff's organization are similar to those in place at many companies, and those companies are just as vulnerable to the cascading failure that was Jeff's promotion.

STRATEGIES FOR SUCCESSFUL NAVIGATION

My friend's scenario would have turned out better had his

organization invested the time and resources into systematically tying promotions, pay raises, benefits, training, and changes of job duties together. Automated systems are perfect for such integration, as they collect and aggregate data, so once a pay raise or promotion is approved, accrual and benefit information is automatically updated in the payroll system. No guessing games. Jeff would have been paid correctly as soon as his promotion went into effect.

When his organization changes him to a manager class of employee and updates his salary in one system, payroll should be updated, his new rate of paid time off accrual should automatically go into effect, and he should be alerted of his new benefits options. He should have the ability to review the custom information on the company's benefits package—with his cost information immediately available—and the ability to sign up for the benefits right there on his phone. He should have a direct line to someone who understands his benefits and is licensed to compare plans, helping him make the correct choice for his family and to maximize his new compensation package.

The necessary assignment of training should be triggered by his class change, each one assigned onto his online portal. In a modernized company, the training is distributed electronically with videos, documentation, acknowledgments, and tests all available so Jeff and others like him can access them when convenient. HR should be automatically notified when the training is complete. They should also be notified if training isn't complete by a certain deadline so they can follow up to answer questions.

Modern automated systems still leave room and even require HR to have human touches. Rather than rote and repetitive work, though, it can instead be used to make sure the employee both appreciates and understands all the information, compensation, benefits, and training—all of which are areas of heavy investment by the organization.

DEMOTIONS AND DISCIPLINARY ACTIONS

Demotions and disciplinary actions, no matter how justified, almost always appear out of the blue to the employee. Unless you have a systematic way of offering immediate feedback when disciplinary action is warranted, an employee will never feel they deserve a demotion.

PITFALLS IN A NON-MODERNIZED ORGANIZATION

Many times, disciplinary actions and demotions don't accomplish their number one goal: to motivate change. In some non-modernized companies, an employee may get a slap on the wrist or receive only negative feedback with no suggestions for improvement; both approaches address the employee's failure but do little to help prevent them from repeating or to help them to learn from the mistake. Instead, employees in these situations usually wind up hating their jobs or wanting to quit because they feel ostracized, not supported. Of course, some managers are better than others and will do more to make the employee change their behavior without destroying motivation. That's the problem in companies, though. By not systematizing these processes like a modern organization would, there is far too much variance in terms of how the disciplinary problem is evaluated, recorded, and corrected. In other words, sometimes it works; sometimes it doesn't.

STRATEGIES FOR SUCCESSFUL NAVIGATION

When it comes to demotions and disciplinary actions, your HR team should ideally only be involved in big issues because you've invested time establishing standard discipline for smaller offenses. For example, a supervisor should not need to call or email HR to report an employee for being tardy or breaking the dress code. If that is your "system," 90 percent of the time, it won't be applied, or it will only be applied when the supervisor is fed up with or doesn't like a particular employee. Instead, the supervisor should have an easy-to-use system in which she can document such small occurrences—or better, that automatically records many instances—a system that can ultimately be used to affect change in the employee's behavior. If an employee is shown a report that notes he broke the dress code three days in one month, for example, he's more likely to be conscious of his attire moving forward. Worst-case scenario, reports of repeated, small offenses can come in handy should your organization ever face a wrongful termination suit or other backlash.

Significant issues that involve HR should start with an investigation rather than the employee being blindsided with the discipline itself. The investigation should follow a standard process so the results are the same for different employees who have the same issue. When you do determine a course of action, you and the employee's supervisor should sit down with the employee in question to explain what disciplinary steps are being taken and why. The goal, remember, is to generate change so the employee can improve. Motivated employees will want to fix whatever mistake they made and, more importantly, never want to do it again. If your disciplinary action hurts your relationship with the employee to the extent he is not motivated to change his behavior, there's nothing to do but let him go.

CHANGES IN FAMILY STATUS

Changes in family status—that is, any change in a family's situation that affects eligibility for benefits—are common occurrences in the world of HR. Common examples include marriage, divorce, the birth of a child, the retiring of a spouse, and more.

A change in family status is often tied to an emotional event for an employee, whether that emotion is positive or negative. Generally, the employee will call HR to discuss options. These interactions can be stressful. Consider an employee who has just learned she is pregnant, and she wants to know the cost of adding a dependent to her insurance plan. Now, consider an employee who has just discovered that his wife—who holds the insurance for the couple at her job—is divorcing him. He needs to know his options for coverage. In these highly emotional moments, employees are looking for help and reassurance, not homework and unexpected surprises. However, in non-modernized organizations, HR is likely spread too thin to address questions individually and may not have time to do anything more than hand the employees in question paperwork or direct them to an 800 number for more information. It may just be that HR is too busy that exact moment to help them, and the employee is left in limbo for a day or two while HR completes whatever else is on their plate before getting to the employee's issue.

STRATEGIES FOR SUCCESSFUL NAVIGATION

When it comes to ad hoc events, you need to have a system capable of automating data collection, form filling, form submission to various benefits and retirement companies, and payroll changes. If you can't fully automate your system, you should at least dedicate a process to handling them as they come. Your systems should contain *all* the information the employee needs and make that information accessible to them when they need it. That way, they can properly explore their options. That process should include easily accessible forms for employees to complete, a review of those forms before submission, and a system that prompts you to make applicable changes when it comes to payroll or insurance carriers. The biggest benefit of a modernized system is that it also frees up HR's time enough to step in and provide support in an emergency. After all, that easily accessible information, nicely organized and explained, is available to HR as well!

LEAVES AND SABBATICALS

Leaves often stem from maternity, paternity, or the health of an employee or loved one. Sabbaticals, on the other hand, represent extended time off work, generally earned based on merit or tenure.*

PITFALLS IN A NON-MODERNIZED ORGANIZATION

The most common problem with leaves and sabbaticals

---

* Some of our clients offer their employees the option to take a three-month sabbatical after they reach five years of employment. They stipulate the sabbatical must be productive and even partner with local nonprofits to help provide service options for employees. They continue paying them during these months. It's expensive for the organization, but employees are grateful for the opportunity. I personally *love* this benefit and hope more organizations can adopt something similar!

in non-modernized organizations is one you will hear many times in this book: a lapse in communication. Often, employees don't view leaves and sabbaticals as benefits until they're interested in receiving them—a shame, as they should be explained as part of the value offered by the organization from day one. When they are not explained, employees present with myriad questions, and it's not always a quick process for HR to provide answers.

The most common type of leave is maternity leave. Employees often have fear and uncertainty around whether or not they will receive maternity leave, for how long, and whether it will be paid or unpaid. The subsequent back and forth with HR delays the employee's ability to make decisions, and it takes time out of HR's day to discuss a policy that should have been explained during onboarding. Not to mention, the time to learn that only two weeks of your maternity leave will be paid leave is *not* when you are six months pregnant!

STRATEGIES FOR SUCCESSFUL NAVIGATION

Your HR team should convey a message that leaves of absence and sabbaticals, whether for maternity or for climbing Mt. Everest, are company benefits. Take care to also clearly define when and how they can be used so employees see them as value-adds, not as vague policies on paper. In addition, it's important to automate the legal and compliance aspects of leaves of absence and sabbaticals so the requesting processes are as streamlined as possible.

OUT-OF-STATE MOVES

Out-of-state moves can be complicated and have substantial implications for all HR processes, including benefits, taxes, and compliance.

PITFALLS IN A NON-MODERNIZED ORGANIZATION

When an employee moves to another state while maintaining her employment, more changes than just her address. In non-modernized systems, multistate issues can sometimes fall through the cracks. For example, many companies find out about tax and compliance issues long after an employee has already moved. To make matters worse, they're often too busy to create a new Department of Labor account in the new state right away, so they'll put it on the backburner—a move detrimental to both the organization and the employee.

STRATEGIES FOR SUCCESSFUL NAVIGATION

It's helpful to have a system in which employees can immediately alert you to changes in their address. If you note an out-of-state move, make a plan and investigate. Have a resource through which you can rapidly determine what needs to happen when you have an employee in a new state and try to prepare for it or automate as much of that process as possible.

Successfully navigating an out-of-state move goes beyond logistics. You're not just learning about an employee's new physical address—you've been given the opportunity to cement a relationship with that employee and show them your company supports their goals and ambitions. Ask questions about why they moved and anticipate how your department might be able to help. For example, if a work-from-home employee indicates he moved from California to Washington state because his spouse was given a better job opportunity, anticipate questions about the spouse's benefits and how they may interact with those you offer.

THE TAKEAWAY

Ad hoc events happen—there's no way around them. It is important to have a plan in place to handle these particular triggers, not only saving time and resources but building relationships in the process. Remember, every ad hoc trigger is an opportunity to make employees feel great about your company. When you leverage automation, you can capitalize on such opportunities instead of being overwhelmed by them.

GO DEEPER

I'll discuss automation as it relates to ad hoc events more in Part 2. In the meantime, go to **PeopleProcesses.com**, click **Resources**, and select **Common Ad Hoc Issues** for more information and to download a list of some of the most common HR issues that you should be able to address!

OFFBOARDING

SAYING GOODBYE THE RIGHT WAY

The final stage of a company's interaction with an employee is offboarding—when an employee is fired, let go, or leaves voluntarily. The offboarding process consists of two categories: what your company *must* do and what it *should* do.

Non-modernized companies typically address only the musts, but the shoulds are just as important, if not more so.

In this chapter, we'll explore how automated offboarding systems can influence not only a unified HR process but also the health of your organization.

AUDREY'S STORY

Audrey was a standout employee: she was motivated,

came to work early, and got along well with clients and peers. There was only one problem: she wanted to do something else in her organization. She was primarily involved in customer service and sales, but she wanted to move into designing management systems and operations. Her organization was growing, but not fast enough to support someone full time in the role Audrey desired.

Feeling stuck, Audrey began to examine her options. Ultimately, she took a position with a competitor. It was the job she wanted, only with a different company. She let her organization know she was leaving, and they didn't take it well. From the company's perspective, they'd done nothing wrong. They hired Audrey to do a job—a job she excelled at and was well compensated for—and they simply couldn't support her request for a role change at that time. As a result, they didn't feel there were any lessons to be learned from her departure.

Audrey's story represents a common scenario when it comes to how organizations exit employees. The company often views the voluntary termination as a dysfunction of the employee, not the company. Reasons for leaving, however, aren't always as clear-cut as some organizations may like to think. Only 22 percent* of voluntary

---

*   Gallup, Inc. "Turning Around Employee Turnover." Gallup.com. May 08, 2008. Accessed June 17, 2018. https://news.gallup.com/businessjournal/106912/turning-around-your-turnover-problem.aspx.

terminations occur because the employee is going to a higher-paying job.

In fact, many employees who leave their companies today do so with no other job in hand. They are motivated more by their career ambition than salary and are seeking an opportunity in a company or industry where they can feel better connected to the culture and mission.*

THE HR OFFBOARDING EXPERIENCE

Employees can leave or be let go for myriad reasons. From an organizational view, though, the response is relatively uniform: in short, it often sounds like, "Give us your laptop and don't come back."

When an employee leaves a company, whether voluntarily or involuntarily, there are standard actions your HR team must take. For starters, you are required to provide a final paycheck. In California, for example, state law requires a check to be provided immediately. In other states, companies have more flexibility, but the rules are ever-changing. (Over the course of a decade in the field, I've had one client whose employee kept getting paid because the company

---

* The scenarios around involuntary termination are less varied than voluntary situations. The experiences for the employee and employer are different in those cases, as the employee is typically let go or fired for cause, such as a disciplinary problem or consistently poor job performance.

forgot to take him off the payroll—a treat for the employee, but a mess in the long run!)

In addition to payroll, other musts include compliance work to ensure the continuity of COBRA medical and dental insurance, if desired, and the completion of any internal compliance processes necessary to the exit process. Your HR team may collect security badges or access keys, distribute paperwork related to retirement accounts, or distribute unemployment information, if applicable.

OFFBOARDING IN A MODERNIZED COMPANY

Offboarding musts are nonnegotiable, but that doesn't mean you should stop there. Still, many non-modernized companies make that mistake.

Modernized companies, on the other hand, focus on their people processes to create a competitive advantage by putting offboarding systems in place to generate gains for the organization in the marketplace.

Such a feat isn't always easy. As an employer, voluntary exits can feel especially difficult to handle. The departure of quality talent can strike a personal chord with managers, spark a misstep in production, and dampen the overall vibe of the organization. Audrey's story is a real scenario. She worked for my organization, and I felt awful when she left. At the time, I was hurt by her decision to work for a competitor. I let her go without offering support or visiting what we may have done to push her to leave—an agonizing process that eventually happened after we struck up a friendship years later.

Remember, your focus in HR should be designing a system of prevention versus cure. Learn from experience, as I did. In effect, practice predicting the future. Look around and consider the steps that need to occur before the next person quits. Preparation allows you to act rationally when the worst happens.

STREAMLINED TERMINATION POLICIES

Every company should have a documented disciplinary policy in place—a practice made simple in a unified HR system that embraces technology. Whether you embrace automation or not, documented policies around discipline and termination are mission critical, especially when you consider that 12 percent of all small- and medium-sized business will be hit with an employee lawsuit, many of which come from firing someone.[*]

Messy and time-consuming legal battles are never wel-

---

[*] "The 2015 Hiscox Guide to Employee Lawsuits: Employee Change Trends Across the United States." 2015. https://www.hiscox.com/documents/The-2015-Hiscox-Guide-to-Employee-Lawsuits-Employee-charge-trends-across-the-United-States.pdf.

come. Making involuntary termination as gentle as possible reduces the likelihood your ex-employee will sue your organization later.

In addition, treating the situation and the employee with respect makes your remaining employees feel more comfortable seeing a colleague fired or laid off. Employees fear the same fate for themselves, so every effort should be made to provide the most benefit for a departing staff member. For example, if you let a manager go, providing a decent severance package and ensuring she can maintain benefits for a period of time isn't simply a gesture of goodwill. It's a courtesy you extend to ensure your remaining employees don't run for the hills. It's putting people first, and it's good business.

A PRODUCTIVE EXIT INTERVIEW

The exit interview is a key part of both voluntary and involuntary exits. If an employee is leaving voluntarily, your HR team should take that opportunity to gain insight into why. Most companies, like mine (at the time) in Audrey's case, fail to look closely enough at what the departure means for the organization.

For example, if a key salesperson opts to leave your company voluntarily, it's important to learn as much as you can about why. You may learn that he wants to pursue an acting career in New York City, in which case you'll know that his departure probably isn't a poor reflection on your company. However, it's still an opportunity to engage in a discussion about your organization and how it can do better. An exit interview is a unique and powerful time to gather perspective. To forfeit such potential would be a missed opportunity. When else are you going to be able to get the unvarnished truth from your employees about what your organization is doing wrong without any fear of retaliation or making someone unhappy?

Knowledge is power, in life and in HR. Employees leave voluntarily for many reasons: pursuing dreams, better pay, other career interests, or because of problems with the organization itself, perhaps a supervisor or company policy. Whatever the case, take the time to do an in-depth exit interview. Perhaps you will gain information that can help the organization succeed in the future.

Once you've gathered feedback, make it actionable by asking the following of yourself and your company: What is missing from your processes that contributed to the departure and prevented the employee from communicating issues or concerns earlier on?

Remember, the entire purpose of leveraging automation and technology is so your HR team can be a force multiplier for the organization to make its people better. When employees choose to leave, it makes sense to be reflective about what processes you can change or implement to address their grievances so the next employee doesn't face the same difficulties or roadblocks.

Another thing to think about when examining the reason for an employee's departure is multifaceted: How did the employee get all the way to quitting? Did the employee not feel they could come to HR or their manager with their concerns? Where in the relationship did it become so incommunicative that you weren't able to address their concerns?

In essence, treat offboarding as you would if you were losing a client after six months. With the client, you'd look back over the six-month period and investigate the source of the problem. Was it in implementation? Was there a problem with service?

The same types of questions apply to employees. If you hired an employee who stayed for a year and a half before going to work for your competitor, what did you do wrong? What did you promise that you couldn't deliver? When you brought them on, did you fail to instill enough trust in your organization? Did the employee believe this was a place he could grow and achieve his career goals and then found he couldn't?

PUT INVOLUNTARY EXITS TO WORK

If an employee leaves involuntarily, you should still conduct an exit interview. In these situations, it's less about learning the why behind the departure and more about minimizing damage. Your priority is to complete paperwork and retrieve company data or equipment while making the exchange as pleasant as possible and minimizing the chance of a lawsuit.

Negotiation is the key to involuntary terminations. You may consider offering a severance agreement in exchange for a document signature ensuring the employee will not pursue legal action, if applicable and allowable in your state. In the end, you're trying to soften the blow of an involuntary termination by making sure the employee is taken care of and your organization is protected at the same time.

While you may think your organization doesn't really deal in severance agreements, the most common severance agreement involves PTO or vacation pay. Many organizations will offer to pay any remaining PTO the employee has accrued if they agree to give two weeks' notice. That's a severance agreement.

With an involuntary termination, however, you have more legal risk. Lay out exactly what your organization needs to protect itself, and negotiate with the departing employee to get the proper documents signed. Remember, contracts must have consideration for all sides, so the employee has to get something for signing any severance papers beyond a grim farewell!

Another thing to note is that severance agreements are generally counted against unemployment insurance. If an employee gets sixteen weeks of unemployment pay after you terminate them, you will pay it through your unemployment insurance. But if you give them twelve weeks' severance pay, it will count towards the total, and they'll only be eligible for four weeks of unemployment. You're going to spend the money either way in most cases, so it often makes sense to generate the goodwill by paying the employee directly. Of course, be sure to check with your attorney or benefits advisor on the rules in your particular state.

WHO SHOULD CONDUCT THE EXIT INTERVIEW?

Whether an employee's parting is voluntary or involuntary, one rule stands: choose someone separate from the employee's direct supervisor to conduct the exit interview. Generally, your HR team will be called in to conduct exit interviews. In especially sticky situations, however, get assistance from someone outside the organization, such as your attorney or third-party HR company.

In most cases, hiring an outside party is only necessary

when terminating someone who reports directly to the CEO. Consider a situation in which HR reports to the CEO, and the director of IT also reports directly to the CEO. If there is a volatile relationship between IT and the CEO, it can be difficult for HR to give an unbiased review. If the problems lie with the CEO, HR may feel compelled to gloss over any negatives or not be open to feedback to the extent necessary to learn something from the exit interview. In fact, outside HR help is definitely needed with sexual harassment complaints or compliance issues if we are talking about a direct report to the CEO.

In all cases, be sure to clearly communicate the employee's departure to clients. If the ex-employee had a client-facing role with established relationships, reach out to those clients, notify them of the change, and introduce them to their new contact. Let key players know what's going on, and then shape the message accordingly.

It is also very important to communicate the departure to remaining employees. How you do that depends on the dynamic within your organization. In smaller companies, the entire organization should be informed. In general, however, I emphasize clear communication specifically with direct reports and coworkers. Coworkers in particular are especially critical to communicate with if you wish to control the narrative. Be compassionate in your delivery, don't speak negatively of the ex-employee, and tell remaining team members how and when you plan to fill the vacancy. Make a plan, present it with confidence and empathy, and commit to it. If you are honestly treating the departing employee with respect, your remaining employees will feel it. Remember, investing in your terminated employees, voluntary or not, is truly an investment in the morale of your remaining team!

GO DEEPER

Not sure where to start with an exit interview? Visit **PeopleProcesses.com**, click **Resources**, and download our **Quick Start Exit Interview** guide.

PART TWO

—

THE COMPONENTS OF AN HR SYSTEM

OPTIMIZING EMPLOYEE EXPERIENCE THROUGH AUTOMATION

A WIN-WIN

Onboarding, annual review work, ad hoc HR duties, and offboarding are all supported or managed by HR systems. Deploying strategically arranged and automated systems can put a positive spin on these events and more, improve the workplace experiences for your employees, and grant your HR team the time to nurture your organization's people and mission. To understand how, let's explore how each life-cycle event can be controlled by six different components of an HR system—each with its own focus, design, and goals:

- **Benefits and Compensation.** This component describes the reward employees receive for coming to work. Major medical, dental, vision, retirement, paid time off, and other benefits are often thought of separately from simply salary, but are, in fact, part of one system.
- **Timekeeping, Accrual, and Scheduling.** This component describes the system for keeping track of who worked and when, when they should be working, whether or not they are eligible for time off, and whether or not they took time off.
- **Payroll.** This component describes the terminal system where much of the information flows to ensure accurate monies are paid to employees. It also includes information such as tax withholding data and retirement contributions.
- **Reporting Systems.** This component describes the tools that help your company gain strategic knowledge about your workforce. It generates the tactical information necessary to investigate complaints, reports on the performance of your employees, and helps you track budgets appropriately.
- **Compliance Systems.** This component describes systems built around maintaining compliance with state, local, and federal laws, as well as maintaining related records. These systems provide the guidance and proactive work impetus to implement compliance fixes before internal issues become legal issues.

- **Cultural Communications.** This component describes how you communicate information to employees, from the big-picture direction of the company to softer issues that affect morale.

NON-MODERNIZED HR SYSTEM DISORDER

Non-modernized companies often have HR systems that negatively impact the employee experience, causing tedious workloads to rise and motivation to diminish. Moreover, because no component is an island, lacking in any single component can create a problem in one or all the others.

Most HR departments have many different systems—whether electronic or on paper—that vaguely interact. Yours may be an organization that uses paper applications, requires HR to type data into the payroll system when an employee is hired, uses an electronic system for benefits, and refers to punch time cards when it comes to determining PTO. Such inconsistencies in methodologies create a system disconnect that not only costs time and resources but also keeps your employees from focusing on their work and your HR staff from developing their people.

Another of the biggest pitfalls in archaic HR systems is the existence of paper. If benefits and compensation, timekeeping, payroll, reporting, compliance, or cultural communications systems are built around paper forms and file cabinets, you have a problem. Overreliance on hard-copy forms can create a number of issues, the most basic of which is the tendency for omissions and other human errors.

Imagine that an employee applies for insurance and fills out a stack of paper to cover his spouse and child. Unfortunately, he doesn't have his child's social security number memorized, so he leaves it blank and assumes he will fill in the missing information later. However, he forgets, signs the documents, and sends them off to your HR department.

There are three possible outcomes of this oversight: If your HR team is on the ball, you'll spend time thoroughly reviewing the paperwork, catch the mistake, and return the files to your employee to complete. This is the best-case scenario, although it's highly inefficient. In a second and more likely scenario, the insurance carrier catches the mistake and declines the application. Then, you must contact the employee, gather the missing social security number, and send the document back to the carrier. In most cases, insurance applications take at least two weeks to process, so you can go weeks before the mistake is remedied—a long time for a child to not be fully covered and another time suck for your HR team in fielding concerned calls from the employee. In the worst-case scenario, the insurance carrier doesn't catch the mistake and issues the policy without covering the child. Then, the child gets an ear infection sometime after, and her parents take her to the doctor. As standard, they present their insurance card and co-pay. Two weeks later, the clinic receives notification from the insurance carrier that the child is not covered, so they send a bill requiring payment in full. Everyone, in turn, scrambles—the parents, your HR department, the insurance company—until it becomes a Gordian knot of confusion, all because of a blank field on an application.

In addition to omitted information, paper forms can also contain incorrect information. An applicant's date of birth, for example, might be entered in the date-of-hire field—a critical detail in terms of calculating PTO seniority. Redundant entries are also troublemakers. Consider the number of standard documents that require name, address, date of birth, and social security number. After so many requests for the same information, applicants can begin to slip when it comes to handwriting. More than handwriting suffers; they'll likely lose their engagement with the company and the onboarding process.

It is difficult to completely divorce yourself from paper in the business world, yet doing so is incredibly important to prevent issues like these from cascading out of control. Every little mistake made on paper turns into hours of work for your HR team—or, in small companies, the business owners themselves—leaving key players spending their time dousing fires instead of investing in improving the company. If you can automate processes to make these experiences less redundant, more accurate, and more efficient, you can communicate more effectively and help move the organization forward.

AUTOMATING FOR THE GREATER GOOD

The end goal of automating HR systems is not to automate the HR role itself, but to unify all the employee life-cycle events and components so your HR staff can focus on nurturing the people in your organization.

It's an obvious benefit that automated systems can compensate for errors common to paper forms, as they will automatically flag missing social security numbers or other omissions. Some of the less obvious benefits, however, have to do with attitude rather than tech aptitude. Employee motivation levels change every day. Automation helps keep processes consistent, allowing your HR team to focus on improving the employee experience around life-cycle events and HR systems. In addition, employees are more apt to be motivated to perform in the workplace if they don't feel bogged down by tedious, time-consuming, and often confusing HR tasks. With an automated system in place to remove the drudgework, you can then use cultural communications, incentives, benefits, and compensation to maintain a consistently motivated workforce.

Motivation is not something you do once by giving a bonus or throwing a party at the end of the year. It's something you can nurture every day by focusing on creating consistent, positive interaction with your team. "Motivation is like being clean," is a great and accurate expression. Just like you need to bathe every day, you must also focus on motivating yourself and your employees as part of your daily routine. The more you can remove time-sapping tasks, the easier it is to lather up motivation.

BUILDING AN HR SYSTEM THAT WORKS

There are four main ingredients to a solid, unified HR system that fuels a productive and satisfied workforce: efficiency, scalability, reliability, and compliance.

EFFICIENCY

Whether the system is payroll, benefits, reporting, compliance, or timekeeping, it needs to be effective. The goal of most HR systems is to generate action. In a compliance system, for example, you're trying to teach employees something specific. In a benefits and compensation system, you want to communicate that the employee is appreciated and well compensated for their work.

SCALABILITY

It's imperative to scale your system to match organizational needs. In other words, HR processes need to grow *with* your organization in a way that doesn't cause undue burden to any party or add time to employee life-cycle events. Improving scalability by putting more time and effort into how something is done allows a higher return in the form of a productive and dedicated staff.

RELIABILITY

In addition to effectiveness and scale, HR systems must be consistent. Typically, managers will see things differently than employees, but it is critical for every manager to see, learn, or react in a similar way to the same situation. If the way employees interact with HR, and the organization as a whole, is unreliable, a great deal of information is left to be understood by tribal stories or word of mouth—not a good scenario.

COMPLIANCE

HR systems must also be compliant and include only accurate information. To ensure this, modern HR systems have compliance checks to guarantee employees receive all necessary information related to policy and compliance changes. Those transmissions and specific details, then, are properly recorded.

Automating your HR system—and building one that works—contributes to your ultimate goal: you'll be able to devote time to your company's human capital and leverage employees' workplace satisfaction into a competitive advantage. The statistics are impressive: the cost to replace an employee is huge. It costs 16 percent of the annual salary for high-turnover, low-paying jobs (earning under $30,000 a year). That means it costs $3,328 to replace a ten-dollar-per-hour retail employee. It costs 20 percent of annual salary for midrange positions (earning $30,000 to $50,000 a year). That means the cost to replace a $40k manager would be $8,000. It costs up to 213 percent of annual salary for highly educated executive positions. That means the cost to replace a $100,000 CEO is $213,000.

If you do your job correctly as a company and focus on making your human capital the best they can be, in five years, they will be at the top of their productivity game. At ten years, an employee is worth their weight in gold. Just like most investments, employees provide the greatest benefit the longer you hold on to them!

GO DEEPER

We are now going to dive into each of those components, but before we do, take a minute to go to **PeopleProcesses.com** and subscribe to our podcast. We have updates every week about the best practices, tools, and compliance updates to help you navigate your HR journey. We also interview business leaders and HR tycoons who have stories from which we can all learn. If you would like to be on the podcast, just drop me an **email at rhamy@poplarfinancial.com** with the subject **Podcast Guest** in the subject line, and I'll reach out to you!

BENEFITS AND COMPENSATION

BEYOND THE PAYCHECK

A well-structured benefits and compensation system interacts seamlessly with employee life-cycle events and other HR components to gauge a job's value to both the company and the employee. Contrary to many approaches, outside of tax treatment, there should be no difference between benefits and compensation.

Some organizations differentiate between wages, insurance, and retirement, but they're all about maximizing an employee's perception of why they come to work and what their reward is, expressed in monetary form. It *is* true, however, that there is a perception component to benefits and compensation that is disconnected from the dollar amount, so it's important to build a system in which both the dollars you spend—and their overall value to the employee—are appropriate and clearly communicated.

A ROBUST BENEFITS AND COMPENSATION SYSTEM

Your benefits and compensation system should gather and present information so you can make good decisions about what you pay your employees. Surprisingly, this isn't always a priority in non-modernized companies.

For a moment, think about how much money your organization has spent learning about and researching your product or service. Whether you're a nonprofit, a for-profit, or a government organization, consider the amount of training time and investment you've allocated to discovering how to most efficiently deliver your process. Now, compare that to the market research, investment, and training you invest in determining how to allocate your largest budgetary items—salaries, benefits, and compensation. If yours is like most companies, you dedicate a significant amount of time, labor, and money to products and services, but you make little effort to make heads or tails of the effectiveness of your benefits and compensation plans or to understand where they fall comparatively in the market.

RECOGNIZING A JOB'S MARKET VALUE

A solid benefits and compensation system helps you

understand the market value of the job being performed. With a thorough system, you can research what other companies are paying for each individual job in your organization instead of simply taking a shot in the dark.

To get a handle on what salary is competitive in your market, you can request a compensation analysis for a fraction of what you pay the employee. Information on what similar companies are paying for major medical, dental, vision, and retirement can go a long way when it comes to retention. If you have an employee in your organization who is excelling, reviewing the compensation analysis may lead you to realize that giving them a 5 percent raise this year makes you competitive in the market and encourages the employee to stay. In that case, you got an amazing return on your money!*

GAUGING EMPLOYEE SATISFACTION AND PERFORMANCE LEVELS

Besides communicating the market value of a particular job, your benefits and compensation system should also be able to provide information about an employee's satisfaction and performance levels—again, tied to the annual review work. If your employees are performing 15

---

* One thing to note: it is much more difficult to value a new hire with a comparison analysis because there's a risk premium involved. You don't know how an employee will perform until they've been with your company for some time. Keeping good people is always a better investment than rolling the dice on a replacement!

percent better on average, producing more, and are more satisfied than others in the industry doing the same job, then you have a clear competitive advantage.

One way to gather such data on outside companies is through detailed survey work, either completed internally or purchased through outside resources. I don't recommend completing the work on your own, as it can be costly and time-consuming. Instead, you can hire third parties to create surveys for you and generate the information you need, and learn the three keys to compensation comparison: average pay ranges, the cost of the benefits, and policies around time off and bonuses.

These details allow you to design a comprehensive benefits and compensation plan for the jobs in your organization that lets you retain and attract top talent!

HARNESSING THE INSIGHT OF BENEFITS AND COMPENSATION

Intelligently gathered and utilized, employee benefits and compensation data can provide valuable insight into other systemic problems.

For example, say an employee is doing well and you're paying her well for it, but she is dissatisfied with her job. By paying well, you've eliminated the compensation factor for dissatisfaction and can redirect your attention elsewhere to solve the problem. Most small business owners know their employees and have a pretty good idea of whether or not those employees are satisfied. However, if those employees are not satisfied, those owners are much less clear on the whys of that dissatisfaction. A strong understanding of the market and a robust benefits and compensation system is your starting point to eliminate what most small businesses think is the problem: that they don't pay enough.

In another example, an employee in Company A thinks he is underpaid but is unfamiliar with salaries in other industry sectors. Approaching his manager with his concern, the employee learns he is actually paid 10 percent above median. At the outset, this information overcomes one issue and alleviates some of the employee's negativity. They know the reason for dissatisfaction is not actually due to lower pay, and both parties can move past that and focus on other factors that may be contributing to dissatisfaction.

DOING MORE FOR LESS

You may review the market information on benefits and compensation and realize your company simply can't afford to pay your employees what they may make elsewhere. If the average pay for the same position in a similar organizations—one your size and in your area—is $10,000 higher annually, you might not be able to meet that figure. This is a common small business concern, as larger businesses have developed the scope to pay people market average or better. The problem in this case is not benefits and compensation, but efficiency. The employees you have, due to your company's systems and organizational makeup in a broader sense, are not generating as much gross revenue as your competitors.

If you realize your company earns less than the average, you have to be creative to retain good talent. Do the uncommon to encourage a positive vibe in your company. Give your staff a premium beyond dollars and cents. Many small businesses thrive in a palpable family atmosphere. The executive director invites staff over for barbeque. They offer a flexible work schedule, extended leaves, and a host of other incentives that don't necessarily cost much but extend a great deal of goodwill. Knowing you can offer those kinds of benefits allows you to view your company through a logical eye and confidently compete for quality staff.

In my company, we've had nonprofit clients who show that their pay is a bit lower than similar organizations, but they shine in their cultural communications and manage to have very low turnover. If you're up front about what you can offer both financially and as an organization, you can help your employees make an informed decision about their place in your company, and you can find ways to retain your best people. Besides, nothing attracts new employees when you need them like happy employees who have been with you for a while!

THE BENEFITS AND COMPENSATION EFFECT

An additional important aspect of benefits and compensation is to recognize its true form and application. If you're an organization that cannot afford to offer platinum-level insurance plans, invest in ensuring the way you communicate your benefits is top-tier. Doing so will dramatically increase your employees' appreciation and understanding of what you offer.

Communicating invisible benefits—those benefits that many employees don't think about because they don't use them every day—is a good place to start. Does your company provide a long-term disability policy or similar benefit? Those plans cost your organization money, and you likely keep them in place a long time in case an employee is sick or injured. Communicate the value of that plan from the beginning, and employees will understand it is a major benefit of working for your organization. Fail to communicate it properly, and they may not even know it exists—a waste of your investment.

GO DEEPER

Now, I know getting this information is sometimes problematic, and my company provides this information for many companies. If you're reading this book, I'll be happy to provide a good starting benefits and compensation report for any job title, in your city, for an organization your size and type. To get yours, go to **PeopleProcesses.com**, click **Resources**, click **Salary Research**, and fill out the short form. I'll email you the report!

TIMEKEEPING, ACCRUALS, AND SCHEDULING

DON'T PHONE IN FUNDAMENTALS

Timekeeping is an important and versatile HR component for two reasons: it is clearly needed to control labor costs for hourly employees, and it's also an opportunity for companies to provide understanding and justification for labor costs of salaried employees.

Timekeeping is comprised of an array of elements—many of which are built around legal compliance—and there are a number of important laws of which every HR team member or business owner should be aware.

The most important regulation concerning timekeeping

is the Fair Labor Standards Act (FLSA), enacted in 1938. In general, the act states hourly employees must be paid a minimum wage and overtime. This labor legislation was the beginning of the forty-hour work week in the United States. Although state minimum wage rates and overtime regulations have fluctuated over the years, the basic Fair Labor Standard of the forty-hour workweek, all work being compensated, and a minimum wage has remained the cornerstone of the labor relationship in the United States.

Your primary tool for maintaining FLSA compliance will be your timekeeping system. You may have employees whose time is not tracked in your timekeeping system. You may have decided that those employees are "exempt" from the FLSA. Whether an employee is legally exempt from the FLSA is beyond the scope of this book. Having said that, the HR system you create (addressed in the last part of this book) should include a clearly stated process for properly classifying all employees in your organization.

FLSA language states wages must be paid if hourly employees are "suffered or permitted to work." It doesn't matter if your employee handbook says overtime must be approved in advance. If your receptionist comes in thirty minutes early every day and leaves thirty minutes late, but never tracks her time, your company is responsible for paying all the hours she worked, period. Of course, as long as she is happy with your company, such a small discrepancy likely won't be an issue. If she is terminated or otherwise becomes surly, however, she can sue you for that money. This scenario is very common, and it's one more reason keeping accurate records is imperative to protecting your organization—a topic I'll explore in detail in chapter 9.

TIMEKEEPING IS IMPORTANT...EVEN FOR YOU, SALARIED SUE

Timekeeping is critical, even for those exempt from the FLSA law. To illustrate this point, imagine a small, non-profit organization that does community outreach support for women. Because nearly everyone in the organization is salaried, they're technically FLSA exempt. As a result, staff initially didn't clock in and out at all.

Most of the staff in this nonprofit were paid the same, but Lisa felt as though she constantly picked up the slack for her coworkers. She felt she continually came in early, did more, and even worked evenings from home to pick up slack. Leaders of the organization knew Lisa was a good employee, but they had no way to verify whether or not she was covering for other people—that is, before they implemented a timekeeping system. When the organization required everyone to track their hours, even though all employees were salaried, they were able to see that Lisa truly was doing more than her fair share.

In sum, tracking your employees' hours, even if they're FLSA exempt, provides information that allows you to judge whether or not they are pulling their weight or are overworked. As a general rule, *everyone* in an organization should clock in and out—even the CEO—to prove the company meets minimum wage and overtime requirements for those covered by FLSA but also to glean information on salaried employees' hours and work routines.

TRACKING THE OVERWORKED EMPLOYEE

Timekeeping addresses the need to make the employee or systems more efficient. If the employee is overworked, perhaps the position should be split between two people. If Carrie is doing great work, but is putting in sixty or seventy hours a week to get it done, without a timekeeping system in place, you may not notice how overworked she is until she leaves your organization. Timekeeping provides insight into labor costs for hourly employees and work production related to time for salaried employees.

In an HR role, this information allows you to determine if you need to add staff or if a particular employee needs to take some time off. Personally, I believe many HR associates, like you, should relate to this point. In many organizations, HR team members are overwhelmed with work, care deeply about the company, and work far too many hours in stressful, deadline-driven environments. Since they are often categorized as FLSA exempt, their long hours are not often obvious to C-level executives. It's hard to keep that pace forever, and attempting to do so can eventually breed resentment and unrest. There is nothing like an hourly employee complaining about having to work overtime (at 1.5 × pay) to a salaried HR manager who works fifty-plus hours every week for the same pay.

TRACKING AND TRENDS

It's just as possible to find an employee who is underworked as it is to find one who is overworked. If Jack earns a salary but comes in late, takes long lunches, and leaves early, that is information you can use. Even if Jack is uber-productive and you don't care about his hours as long as the job gets done, the timekeeping spotlight reveals his job is one that can be done quickly. This information is useful when determining compensation and advertising for future positions.

Timekeeping can also be useful to identify trends in your market or organization—another helpful bit of information when it comes to forecasting and future planning. At Poplar Financial, a huge amount of work flows in around

December and January. Without timekeeping in place, we may have trouble quantifying this trend and just think we work all day, every day, forever—which can be what it feels like! However, because we utilize a timekeeping system, we can understand and plan for the time and labor commitment we will need to handle future busy seasons.

FLSA-EXEMPT TIMEKEEPING

Convincing managers, executives, or FLSA-exempt staff to clock in is a hard sell, but it sets an example throughout the company. Employees working hourly often wonder if the salaried personnel put in as many hours as they do. It can be difficult for managers to enforce timekeeping when they haven't done it themselves. Because it shows the time spent by each employee, tracking hours in the upper ranks is an effective way to boost morale and transparency.

Implementing this practice in a company is no easy task. In tenured organizations, staff have likely been salaried for years and work all hours of the night. Your system needs to be flexible enough to handle a variety of situations—a step that requires patience and understanding. It may have been twenty years since a staff member has ever physically clocked in and out, so you will likely get pushback when it comes time for implementation. However, if the policy is company-wide—that is, from the CEO down—employees are more likely to understand the change is about unifying

HR systems for long-term company benefit, not about catching them doing something wrong.

TIMEKEEPING SYSTEMS AT A GLANCE

Three types of timekeeping systems are commonly used in today's workplace. Each has varying levels of complexity, advantages, and disadvantages.

MANUAL, PAPER-BASED SYSTEMS

Manual systems are the most basic for timekeeping and, ultimately, are nearly ineffective in their simplicity. Sliding a paper card into a modified clock that stamps the time was the height of modern technology in the 1930s, and many companies still use them today. Some small businesses' time tracking hearkens to the 1700s, and employees actually *hand write* their time on a ledger or calendar book. It's the "I got here at 8:00. I promise" method.

When HR has employees' time information, they enter it into a payroll system manually. In the sub-fifty-employees market, many companies still use this method. Not surprisingly, there are multiple points of failure and a high degree of inaccuracy in this approach. Employees tend to omit details: perhaps they forgot to clock out one day, didn't sign the book, or didn't fill the time card out until the end of the week. At the end of the pay period, HR winds up with a large stack of time cards and PTO requests on paper, and they must spend hours typing it all into the system.

ELECTRONIC TIMEKEEPING SYSTEMS

The next level above paper systems is electronic time-keeping, often known as web clocks, where employees are able to clock in and out on a computer. The employee and supervisor can review the hours for accuracy before submitting. Most systems have a way of alerting employees if they forgot to clock in or out and generally also provide a scheduling component. Ultimately, electronic timekeeping systems allow employees to review past work history, examine their current work schedule, and request time off—a big step up from paper systems, all without a drastic increase in complexity.

For security, these online systems can be locked down easily. This way, your employees can only clock in and out from a computer that is on your company's network.

PHYSICAL ELECTRONIC SYSTEMS

Physical electronic systems utilize a keycard or ID tag which allows employees to clock in and out. Employees can access, review, and approve their time entries on a computer or other device, such as a smartphone. This route is much less work for employees, especially if they are not particularly technologically savvy, since they pretty much don't have to remember a username or password.

Biometric systems like fingerprint and iris scanners are also becoming more and more common. There are many advantages to this suite of tools—the biggest of which is that there's nothing for an employee to misplace! You can lose a keycard, but it's far more difficult to lose your finger. They're also great for factories or other locations where dangling cards or straps can be a safety problem. Biometric systems are more expensive and do require time to set up, but they save time and money in the long run.

A TIMEKEEPING SYSTEM'S ROLE IN REDUCING FRAUD

Timekeeping provides accurate data to better understand employee roles and labor costs, but it does more than that too: it's a reliable tracking system that helps reduce fraud.

There is a great deal of fraud in timekeeping. One of the most common is buddy punching, a situation in which a coworker clocks another in and out. The other is outright lying—that is, when an employee says she was at work when she wasn't. Ask yourself this question: if your organization uses paper time sheets and you show up at 8:05 three days in a row, are you going to write down 8:05 or

8:00? Most of us would simply choose the latter. Sometimes, an employee might "forget" he took an extra thirty minutes for his lunch break, or he may leave at 4:45 on a Friday and write 5:00 in the time log. Not surprisingly, paper time sheets are, by far, the least secure.

Clocking in and out online with a username and password is more secure, since many employees don't want to share login information because there might be ancillary data on their profile they don't want a fellow employee to have. Most online systems are set up to only allow the employee to "clock in" or "clock out" and, therefore, not have the ability to overestimate their time worked. Buddy punching, however, can still occur on an electronic system if employees do opt to share login information. In general, however, it is much more difficult to say you left later or came in earlier if you're using electronic systems.

Physical keycards, like RFID tags (similar to the key fobs you probably use to get into your gym) greatly reduce fraud, due in most part to required pre-planning. It's similar to gearing up for a heist: conspirators must arrange to pass ID tags to a main player, do the job, and reverse the routine after the getaway. This isn't a movie scene; it's real life. One of my manufacturing clients once had a Saturday morning shift that started at 8:00 a.m., and the CEO didn't check on it often. For many months, they ran a schedule with four employees on the shift, including an assistant manager. On Fridays, one of them would collect the others' ID cards. The "point man" would show up to work at 8:00, clock them all in, and the rest would wander in around 9:30 or 10:00. This went on for months, and it was not at all obvious to the employer. Eventually, pure luck brought him to the plant on a Saturday morning to check on an order that was supposed to go out Friday. Despite everyone being clocked in, only one person was there working. No other trucks were in the parking lot, and the owner rapidly realized what happened. Good systems prevent this kind of fraud.

The best timekeeping method for fraud prevention, of course, is to deploy a biometric system. A group of hooligans can't give their thumbs to someone to clock in for them, so that eliminates buddy punching or clocking out fifteen minutes early. Biometric clocks record all the necessary data and will save you more than the cost of the system.

BONUS FUNCTIONS OF ELECTRONIC TIMEKEEPING SYSTEMS

A solid timekeeping system handles your black-and-white time tracking, but it should also track accruals. In the same place employees go to clock in and out, they should be able to check their PTO status, look at their available paid sick days, and see if they're eligible to schedule vacation.

Timekeeping and PTO should be directly integrated, especially because many employees take unplanned time off, such as when they're ill. This information should be stored and kept current in a place both the employee and manager can access. The system should also be able to track how much PTO an employee receives, depending on their tenure and job title. It should automatically calculate available time and give the employee the ability to request time off in the future, approve it through their supervisor, and have it reflected on their schedule.

In addition to accruals, an electronic system should also address scheduling. At its most basic, it should assign schedules to groups of employees with certain attributes. In a restaurant, for example, a weeknight shift at a diner may require five waitresses, a chef, three bus boys, and two hosts. A weekday shift, however, may require fewer employees. The electronic system should know your labor needs and generate a schedule around them, the benefits of which go beyond job title.

Your system should be able to track not just who's working or who will work but also attributes specific to those employees—such as who in a daycare center is CPR certified or who in a hospital is licensed to perform certain procedures.

In addition, a good scheduling system should not only

allow you to create a detailed schedule but also an action plan when the schedule isn't followed, thereby eliminating the possibility of being short-staffed or unnecessarily over-spending on staff. It should be able to communicate with the missing employee, their manager, and even alternative staff who could pick up the shift in a pinch when someone doesn't show. These more advanced functions, depending on the size and type of your organization, are huge time-savers. They will often more than justify their cost.

TIMEKEEPING AND PAYROLL MAKE A CONNECTION

It is quite common for timekeeping scheduling systems to be completely separate from payroll. Paper systems are obviously separate, and even electronic systems often stand alone, but the best systems directly integrate payroll and timekeeping. In these environments, when the pay period is over, all hours go straight into payroll. All your HR team has to do is manage the timekeeping side and make sure the hours entered are correct.

Nonintegrated systems cost more money and take more time because staff must manually move information, leaving room for errors. Consider a company with forty employees. In this office, one HR staff member enters the information for each employee, whether from a paper reading or a report, twenty-six times a year. That's a thousand occasions to make a mistake. It will happen, and it can be costly.

A robust, integrated system is not only more efficient, but it also provides more information when it comes time for annual reviews: reports showing absences and tardies, utilization of PTO, schedule shifts, hourly labor or salaried expected hours, and more. The data is there for the employee and supervisor to review; nothing is based on gut feelings or mindless ratings.

A system needs to provide data to support ad hoc duties as well. Timekeeping will be a great help in managing long leaves and sabbaticals. It should also be customizable to handle new regulations related to a change of state, such as a change in the way overtime is calculated. Overall, the system needs to be flexible and connected enough such that all changes are reflected appropriately in every category, including timekeeping.

MAKING OFFBOARDING EASIER

When it comes to timekeeping and offboarding, a unified system should make it simple and quick to lock a terminated employee out while simultaneously keeping and storing records within the platform or program. Compare this to the same process in a paper system. In this archaic approach, if you're called to access the work history of a terminated employee, you will likely visit a file to sift through hundreds of papers and timecards. With an electronic system, however, you can generate a report showing every time an employee clocked in and out, every time he approved his own hours, every supervisor note, etc.—all in a matter of seconds, not days.

GO DEEPER

For resources and helpful information regarding timekeeping, accruals, and scheduling, visit **PeopleProcesses.com**, click **Resources**, and download our **How to Reduce Labor Costs without Compromising Quality Checklist.**

PAYROLL

WHERE IT ALL COMES TOGETHER

Like all components of an HR system, payroll should interact seamlessly with other HR processes. A relatively long-lived nonprofit client with around fifty employees is a phenomenal example of an organization for which this strategy worked. In the past, they used paper-based time sheets in the form of a booklet at the front desk. When employees arrived, they signed the booklet under the watchful eye of the receptionist. This timekeeping process was repeated during lunch breaks and at the end of the day. At the conclusion of every two-week pay period, employees had to individually prepare a time sheet and hand it in to their supervisor, who then turned around and delivered it all to HR.

Their whole world changed when they switched to an automated system. Employees are now able to review their hours and request time off through an online platform, and all necessary information feeds into tables that inform other HR processes.

Previously, every time payroll came around, HR had to chase down missing timecards. They also had to determine if anyone took time off and may have failed to provide a paper record of same. Then, they had to review any salary changes. If supervisors had a comment about any timekeeping piece, they would scribble it on the already crowded form. After the arduous and time-consuming process of gathering all the necessary data, HR then had to key it into their antiquated payroll system—another painstaking process, as they utilized different pay codes and paid employees different amounts depending on department and tenure.

In general, it took a full-time HR team member about two days to gather the necessary information and key it all into payroll. Now, it takes no time. The system does it automatically.

WHY IS PAYROLL SO IMPORTANT?

Every HR system feeds into payroll: benefits, compensation, timekeeping, accruals, compliance, and onboarding and offboarding systems. In fact, payroll is the end point for all these pieces. By automating or modernizing these individual components, you can greatly improve your payroll processes. Like my client, your company transforms from manually collecting a slew of data on a recurring basis and spending hours reviewing it to simply opening a fully integrated system with the same information—and much more—available in seconds.

Payroll prep work saves a recurring administrative burden. All your information from timekeeping to W-4 details are already included and cross-checked, timekeeping checks have been done at the employee and supervisor levels, and benefits enrollment has been confirmed. Each component that can make payroll complicated is handled individually and funneled to a central location. If integration is done correctly, it takes nearly no time at all to run payroll. In fact, 80 percent of our clients with an average staff size of sixty-six complete payroll in less than five minutes.

AN EFFECTIVE AUTOMATED PAYROLL SYSTEM

A robust payroll system is made of a handful of key characteristics that should be considered in relation to your company's specific needs.

- The system needs to be complicated to set up but easy to run, taking into account every variable relevant to your organization. There are hundreds of payroll vendors and software packages available today. Search for a system that places its focus on setup and, once done, runs in seconds. Some systems claim they are "easy to use," but if anything is even remotely off or different, they crumble under the pressure. Be aware.

- The system should have flexibility and be customizable to your company's needs. For example, a nonprofit may need different accounting functions, a manufacturing environment may pay based on the number of widgets produced, or a construction company may need variable hourly rates depending on job type. Find a system that handles complexities your organization will face, and design it correctly from the beginning.
- The system should interface with other key HR systems—timekeeping, benefits and compensation, etc. You can't afford to manually pull other components and bring them over to payroll. Doing so kills your productivity and increases the likelihood of errors.
- The system should be integrated into the onboarding process. In many non-modernized systems or companies, this isn't the case. Employees are onboarded but are not entered into payroll until their first payday, which may be four weeks from their hire date. Payroll details should be addressed immediately so that information can be accurately entered and double-checked by the employee as part of a streamlined process.
- The system should be accurate—and most are. In particular, the system should be able to calculate deductions, taxes, and garnishments accurately.

Child support orders, for example, are highly complex, and many payroll systems cannot automatically handle them. A common child support order might indicate the employee is required to pay 50 percent of his gross wages to the child support order, as long as he's making more than ten dollars per hour and works more than twenty hours per week. If he has a second child support order, the orders should be split equally. If he has a bankruptcy order, it can never exceed removal of 25 percent of his pay. Layering, prioritizing, and structuring garnishment orders can clearly get complicated, but your system must be able to perform this task.

- The system should allow employees to check their tax forms and review check stubs, preferably online so they can have access to this critical information on their device of choice without taking up HR's valuable time.
- The system should have the ability to handle special features, such as multiple pay rates, job codes, split department accounting, and withholding methods.
- The system should be able to automate the payroll approval process with an easily accessible, multiplatform method, preferably with a two- or even three-tier approval system for HR.

PAYROLL'S LINK TO LIFE-CYCLE EVENTS

Your payroll system isn't all about numbers; your employees interact with it too. Their first encounter with payroll is during onboarding, as this is generally the time they'll provide direct deposit information and withholding instructions. The process should be simple. The employee shouldn't have to review their handbook in one system, learn timekeeping requirements in another platform, and then go somewhere else to provide HR with financial information. All these actions should be integrated and tied to one system that talks directly to payroll.

Payroll also has an important role to play in annual reviews, as it should provide accurate information and reporting for the year—a key benefit, as it allows you to set budgets and holistically understand compensation. This strategic information helps you make key decisions about departmental funding, individual funding, pay raises, and bonuses from an individual to a company level.

For ad hoc changes—promotions, pay raises, out-of-state moves, changing of deductions, and more—the payroll system should be set up so it takes only seconds and minimal clicks to make changes. The process around changing states can be created such that you need only input the move date, and the rest is taken care of automatically.

Finally, offboarding should be as smooth as onboarding

when it comes to payroll and all other systems. When an employee leaves, whether voluntarily or involuntarily, payroll should be easy to lock down so the employee does not accidentally keep getting paid. The system should also save those records indefinitely, or at least for seven years. Because everything ties to payroll, offboarding in one system must shut down timekeeping, accrual, scheduling, benefits, and more.

Such a system benefits your ex-employee and your organization for a number of reasons, as errors in benefits shut down sometimes come back to haunt both of you. While an ex-employee might have their benefits terminated immediately, you might forget to inform the voluntary accident insurance carrier, dental insurance carrier, or any of the countless vendors who need to be notified. When these tasks are completed in one system, all parties are made aware with one cascading alert—saving hassle for everyone involved.

GO DEEPER

To learn more about how to optimize payroll, visit **PeopleProcesses.com,** click **Resources,** and download the **Payroll Manager's Per-Payroll Checklist** to get started with your current system!

REPORTING SYSTEMS

DATA IS THE DRIVER

In 2016 Specialty Home Care, a home healthcare organization, saw its staff reach eighty full-time employees. That same year, the Affordable Care Act (also known as "the ACA," "Obamacare," "Thanks, Obama," "I blame Obama," "C'mon, relax you guys," or "We're all fine here now") required all employers with more than fifty employees to offer affordable insurance coverage. In 2015 ACA benefits were not required unless a company had one hundred or more employees.

Specialty Home Care had reviewed their numbers in 2014 and confirmed they did not have to offer ACA benefits. Two years later, the requirement applied to them, and the penalty for noncompliance was around $3,000 per employee.

The organization came to Poplar Financial for assistance, and we helped them move into 2016 in full compliance using a new robust reporting system. Then, in January of 2018, they received a notice indicating they did not provide adequate health insurance in 2015. Their proposed penalty was $529,000, and they had fourteen days to reply with confirmation or to object to the penalty and provide all supporting documentation.

A half-million-dollar bill is never the best way to start the year. Specialty Home Care was confident they should not have to pay the penalty, but now they had to prove it—a task that would have been much easier had the robust reporting system been in place during the year in question.

A POWERFUL TOOL

The tax penalty assessed to the healthcare company originated from a decision they made three-and-a-half years prior. At the time, their systems were based with a major payroll company that provided applicable information. However, that information was not stored in a searchable or reportable way. After four years of payroll documentation for nearly two hundred employees, the company had 2,200 pages of "proof" that then needed to be sorted and summarized.

Specialty Home Care worked around the clock to comply

with the request in the allotted time, and they struggled because the expertise required to do so was beyond their scope. In the end, the company spent approximately $10,000 in outside counsel—and two weeks of productivity for much of their administrative staff—to turn the pages into a usable, organized spreadsheet they could submit to the government. If the organization had a compliance system in place like they have now, they could have generated a response in less than five minutes.

Reporting systems do more than collect and keep data; they also generate reports you need to make good decisions, help prove compliance, and assist in answering any complaints. Let's explore how this works—and why it's so important.

PROOF ON DEMAND

A substantial component of successful business operations is the ability to provide proof on demand that you and your employees have done your job right. Automated reporting helps accomplish this imperative, providing tangible, accurate evidence of actions and information surrounding payroll, timekeeping, and PTO. It also keeps track of critical dates and data surrounding benefits, compensation, and trainings. As most HR people know, it's not enough to just state a policy; you must train your people to comply with it. Beyond that, it's not enough to just train your people, you have to be able to prove you did it correctly and in a timely fashion.

A reporting system needs to show employees' authorization for benefits deductions, evidence that you offered the benefits, and if or why they were declined. In this way, if an employee is diagnosed with cancer three months after open enrollment but opted out of health insurance at the time, she cannot come back and say she had no knowledge of such a policy. Similarly, your reporting system should also be able to prove you complied with laws—such as COBRA—after an employee leaves your company. In these instances and others, reporting covers your organization when it counts.

REPORTING WAGE AND HOUR COMPLIANCE

Reporting systems should also be tied to timekeeping because it's necessary to prove wage and hour compliance. Reporting systems can verify when an employee was working and when they were not, whether the employee accepted their hours as correct, and whether they were paid correctly based on those hours. In addition, reporting systems can assist in proving a company's fiscal responsibility by showing there is a method by which fraud can be prevented.

In relation to wages, payroll reporting needs to integrate

directly into your accounting system's general ledger, or at least provide an easy method by which accounting information is entered. This allows your HR team to track funds on a per-pay basis or by expense. By moving payroll into an accounting system, that reporting function allows a third-party company (or your CPA) to audit the information quickly.

The payroll reporting system should take care of all the granular details related to tracking beyond simply how much you spent on payroll and taxes. It should dig to the nitty-gritty level of data—all the way down to the amount of employer contribution per benefit, per person, per department.

EFFICIENCIES FOR ONBOARDING

Reporting systems are also part of onboarding. When employees are brought on, and they sign nondisclosure agreements, complete emergency contact information, and fill out their employee handbook receipt, your reporting system must have the capability to quickly show when these tasks were completed, including dates and signatures.

In addition, your reporting system should also efficiently track employees' trainings and certifications, as well as their renewal dates. It's true that having this information accessible allows you to stay compliant and up to date, but the key function of a reporting system is to help you rapidly respond to notices—whether from the Department of Labor, the ACA, IRS, or any other entity.

STRATEGIC BENEFITS OF AUTOMATED REPORTING

Outside of the ability to gather information and respond to problems, reporting systems should also be able to generate strategic data, such as trends in your organization, overall costs per job title, distributed bonuses by department, and more. All these elements blend together inside the HR world to improve your strategy and support you in making the right decisions for your organization. On the whole, the ability to identify trending data by department sets your company up for a profitable and successful future.

ANNUAL REVIEWS

When it's time for annual reviews, in addition to time tracking and overtime, your reporting system should also identify any certificates, licenses, vendors, or benefits that need to be changed or updated. For example, if there is a need for your benefits system to interact with the legacy insurance vendor, your reporting system should generate an enrollment form that can be faxed in, per the outdated requirements of your vendor. It should allow you to see what you will be billed for retirement and insurance offerings, broken down by benefit.

TROUBLESHOOTING

Finally, your reporting system should be a reliable troubleshooter. For example, if employees aren't happy with how an issue was handled, your reporting systems should help you figure out why. Where is the bottleneck in paperwork? What is causing friction in the ranks? If you know an employee went into the system and updated her W-4 information on her own, that allows you to pinpoint where a payroll problem may have occurred.

GO DEEPER

To see if your reporting system makes the cut, visit **PeopleProcesses.com** and go to **Resources**. Download the **HR Reporting Checklist** to run your system through a few common scenarios and see if it has the capabilities you need.

COMPLIANCE
SYSTEMS

PREPARE NOW, SAVE HASSLE LATER

Compliance systems are essential for providing timely updates in regulation changes, and can make all the difference in a company crisis. Consider, for example, how ABC Healthcare stayed on track in the face of impending doom.

ABC Healthcare works in the field of Medicare and Medicaid, and the entirety of their compensation is government-provided at $13.50 per hour. Their full-time staff ranges from 200 to 250 at any given time, and they have another 300 part-time employees. On average, they hire about 150 people a month because the turnover rate in the industry is roughly 400 percent. The company can only pay their employees around nine dollars an hour, leaving $4.50 per hour per employee to run the rest of the company.

ABC Healthcare's sheer number of staff greatly increases the risk of having a disgruntled employee or two. It is common knowledge that the more employees you interview and hire—and the more complex your situation—the higher your odds of receiving a complaint from a regulatory authority or lawyer. In ABC Healthcare's case, an employee complained to the Department of Labor and cited unfair hiring practices. She claimed the company was discriminatory and that she wasn't hired for a race-related issue.

One day, without warning, two Department of Labor auditors strolled into ABC Healthcare's doors and announced the company was under a review for compliance. On the spot, the auditors asked to see the company's hiring records, a list of all questions asked on the employment application, the full employee handbook, and a complete list of onboarding processes. In addition, they also asked to review a few recent interviews in their entirety.

Although surprised by the audit, the HR and executive team at ABC Healthcare were not worried. They had conducted 150 interviews that month, so there was no shortage of interviews to review. More importantly, the company had a compliance system in place that allowed them to quickly and efficiently show the following: who had applied for jobs, who had been hired, how interviews were conducted, what information was provided at onboarding, what documents were signed (by whom and when), what trainings were required and completed (per person and per role), and all manager actions for every department. In addition, the practices and policies of the company were at their fingertips and easily shared with the auditors.

An unannounced auditor visit to most companies with that kind of turnover would have HR teams and business owners sweating bullets and nursing ulcers. Without proof to back up claims, you're often up a creek with no option but to hire expensive lawyers and hope the business survives. In ABC Healthcare's case, an audit that could have taken months took two days, and they were cleared of any wrongdoing. Crisis averted.

HR'S BEST FRIEND

A compliance system allows your HR team to address issues quickly and proactively—even those that are constantly in flux. Every state has compliance regulations which are continually changing, and federal labor laws are often amended. For example, Tennessee recently changed the language of required notices, which all employers must provide to employees. Between federal and state changes, those required notices have changed four times in twelve months. Fewer than 10 percent of businesses with under a thousand employees made those changes in a timely manner—a percentage that should, and could, be far higher.

A compliance system is HR's best friend because it helps your company know what has changed, what is changing, and what to do about it. Your team can then stay ahead of the curve and appropriately communicate applicable changes to your employees. You can collect their feedback, signatures, and any complaints in a timely manner—and, of course, track that it was done via a reporting system—so you're able to produce records years down the line. A solid compliance system can help turn a good HR manager into a great one—from someone who cares to someone who cares *and* is actively moving the company forward.

WHAT AUTOMATED COMPLIANCE CAN DO FOR YOU

By definition, automation makes processes run efficiently, and it's no different when it comes to your company's internal compliance system. A well-executed system should know your company policies and procedures and proactively alert you of any issues. There will be times, however, when compliance issues are brought up by employees and not your system. For this reason, it's critical that your system also provides a way for you to do your own research so that you can identify solutions when the situation calls for it.

Besides proactively alerting you and giving you space to form your own opinions, your compliance system should also notify your organization when you've drifted beyond the bounds of established compliance. Many businesses assume there are always concrete parameters to compliance, but that's not true in practice. There are, in fact, many cases on the edge of compliance. More often than not, the government will release a new vague regulation with no specifics about what it truly means. A compliance system should let you know when you're treading too closely to the edge of the gray area, indicating it's time to step away from your internal library, live support, or trainings, and contact an attorney.

COMPLIANCE AUDITS AS ROADMAPS

A compliance system should be capable of handling 99 percent of your compliance issues, but you should also know its limits. Ultimately, your system should point you in the direction to make long-term improvements. Completing internal compliance audits at regular intervals is an important step in moving the organization in that direction.

Our company uses a pair of audit approaches: one is a

quick, ten-question audit to identify any glaring issues, and the other is a more in-depth audit completed over time that allows us to dive into the nitty-gritty of compliance. The quick audit allows us to zoom in on potential problem areas. If we find one, the compliance system provides a roadmap for what we need to do to improve our processes. Once you know if you're facing a compliance issue, the system gives you the information you need so you can make an informed decision about whether or not it's time to call in an expert to help or just take care of it yourself.

QUICK AUDIT QUESTIONS

- Do you know the pre-hire steps you should follow to ensure you don't hire an employee with a poor work or attendance history?

- Have you organized your employee leave programs (ADA, FMLA, return to work, PTO, absenteeism) and communicated them to your employees?

- If you offer employee benefits (voluntary or company-subsidized), are all benefits offered to every employee who is eligible, every year, and do you have records for all enrollments, including declinations signed by each employee?

- Do you have a process to manage employee complaints, discipline, and termination designed to keep you out of court?

COMPLIANCE SYSTEMS FACILITATE EMPLOYEE TRAINING

Many view compliance as simply an excuse for more paperwork. There's some truth to that, as the heart of compliance is documentation. However, true compliance goes far beyond the paper or the screen. For example, simply stating in your policy manual that there is to be no sexual harassment in your organization does not in any way protect you. You have to do more!

To make sure you're covered, you must outline each compliance topic in the manual—whether it's discrimination, harassment, driving safety, active shooter drills, or anything in-between—and teach your employees to *act* in a compliant manner, not just "initial here, please" to prove they've read a paper about how to behave. Your compliance system is your repository for both those documents and training materials.

It's critical that those training materials are robust. If you're conducting training using methods from 1987 by which you invite all of your employees to the lunchroom, slide a clunky tape into a VHS player, and show them a video of someone talking for an hour, you can prove you performed the training, but you know that you truly haven't trained anyone. The entire process performed in this way is incredibly inefficient. Not only will the "training" not affect change, but it is not reliable enough to determine whether your current policies and systems are working.

Instead, employees should receive their training during onboarding or as part of their annual review, ideally in automated settings and viewable on mobile and desktop. Training should go beyond the basics and be interactive, including elements such as video, text, multiple choice questions, and live chat. These elements will inform employees of procedures and behavior expectations in an engaging and memorable way.

Once training is complete, compliance systems should track who took the training and when, and store that information in employee files. Each employee's training history should be saved for the long term, just like other records, and be accessible as needed by the employee, the supervisor, and the department.

Training isn't something that happens only during onboarding. Quite the contrary! Your employees must be trained periodically as requirements shift and your organization adjusts accordingly. Because training on compliance issues is so necessary, it's important to make the employee experience one that's as digestible and accessible as possible. Automating these and other recurring HR events saves you and your team time, and frees you to focus on forming relationships and spearheading positive change in your organization.

At the end of the day, not having the right compliance system is like putting your business on credit cards. It's better to spend your money and get your system properly set up, trainings and all, so you don't face substantial bills down the road—with interest.

GO DEEPER

You can download the full ten-question audit at **PeopleProcesses.com**. Click **Resources** and **Quick HR Audit**.

CULTURAL COMMUNICATION

THE CRUX OF EMPLOYEE ENGAGEMENT

All companies should include a systematic approach to facilitate effective employee communication—a critical element to a successful business. Your organization can offer the best benefits and the best pay in your market, but if you can't communicate that to your employees, it doesn't matter. Communication is the most important component of HR, as it is the multiplier that makes everything you've done work effectively.

A FAILURE TO COMMUNICATE

Consider, for example, WR Manufacturing, a large organization that had a workforce of around three hundred employees for many years. In its early days, the company's benefits offerings weren't the best, as the organization was still finding its footing. Employee insurance plans featured relatively low co-pays for doctor visits ($30) and specialists ($70). Pharmacy co-pays were between $10 and $50, and employees had a $5,000 deductible for hospital visits. They were also on the hook for a high out-of-pocket max of $6,000. Over the years, the policy got worse as co-pays gradually increased. Employees weren't happy with their health plan, the high deductible, and costs, but they didn't hate it either. It was all they knew.

As the company grew and became more profitable, the founder decided he wanted to start taking much better care of his employees. During a particularly successful year, when several smart tech investments paid off, he thought that rather than offer raises and bonuses, he would revolutionize the benefits package. The new plan would have a $2,500 out-of-pocket maximum, of which the company would cover $1,500. Employees, then, were responsible for the first $1,000 in full—co-pays, prescriptions, doctor visits, hospital visits, everything—and nothing after that.

When the switch was announced, WR's founder was devastated to learn that the new benefits plan was not well-received by his employees, despite the fact that the company was spending nearly $2 million per month on benefits—more than doubling their costs. The change would, in fact, cut each employee's insurance costs by as much as 83 percent. So what was the problem? Why weren't the employees happy with the change?

The answer is simple: lack of communication.

Some employees were in for a shock when their first doctor visit was $127 instead of the thirty dollars they paid last year, and they were furious because they had no idea what was going on. Many employees' families had four monthly prescriptions at thirty dollars each. In January, those same prescriptions jumped to $150 each. Furthermore, the new plan required employees to get a debit card so that once they reached their $1,000 limit, they could make other health purchases. However, employees didn't know how to check their balances or time their purchases.

The good news is that by July, the employees had discovered that the plan actually benefited them because most no longer had health costs for the remainder of the year. The bad news is that because the benefits weren't communicated effectively in the first place, the employees' unhappiness soured what was actually a positive event.

COMMUNICATION AT THE HEART

Cultural communication goes to the heart of the employee-employer relationship. Strong communication isn't just warm and fuzzy; it helps employees perform better too. Whether you're conducting a training, conveying a disciplinary action, or even announcing a holiday party, *how* you communicate is just as important as *what* you're communicating.

In a non-modernized company, the extent of communication is usually centered on getting paperwork signed and filed. A company that embraces automation for HR systems, on the other hand, can spend more time packaging communication than they do on the actual distribution. They know automation will take care of distributing, recording, tracking, and collecting documents, so they can focus on strategically designing the "customer" experience, not just signature hunting.

Careful communication is attractive from a cost perspective too. Think about it: costs are generally the same whether you communicate information well or do it poorly, so it behooves you to put some effort into the process of helping your team understand and appreciate what you have to say.

Spending marginally more money and time on the front end is a return on investment. If you expend the cost of complying with a new law, you can spend marginally more to ensure legal compliance *and* the full understanding of your employees. Imagine buying a new $800,000 machine for your company and then skipping the $3,000 training designed to teach your employees how to use it. That's what happens with a lot of HR changes! You are spending big bucks on benefits, salaries, PTO, compliance, and technology, so don't skip out on the marginal cost that makes all of that effective, understood, and appreciated by your staff. Business owners and HR managers recognize the value of a small increase in cost generating a much higher return on investment, and communication is the way to do that.

Improving systems and their execution has a lasting effect in employees' eyes and their performance. Doing it well and in a fun way that establishes a rewarding relationship makes a tremendous difference in how an employee views your organization.

A COMMUNICATION SYSTEM'S BEST FEATURES

We know communication is a key component to success, but how do you evaluate your current system to glean the most benefit? It's imperative to step toward a communication reboot in small, well-planned steps. The final product, of course, should be evergreen while still allowing you to make continual improvements as you grow and gain more value from your interactions with your team members. Let's explore tips for selecting the right communication system.

STAY FLEXIBLE

Your system should be flexible when it comes to benefits, payroll, and compliance, as you never know exactly what information you will need to communicate. If your communication system is a set of seven templates that only allows you to change numbers, your system isn't flexible enough to accommodate future changes. The same applies to in-person meetings: they should be a balance of flexible and systematic, as it's difficult to generate the same experience every time and still find room to improve it.

CONVENIENT, CUSTOMIZED, AND ACCESSIBLE

The best communication system builds from your company's focused time and effort in creation, design, and distribution. Take care to ensure that information is complete, easy to understand, and presented in a way that leaves your employees feeling empowered by their new knowledge, not overwhelmed by it.

Video is the most effective communication tool. If you have a thirty-minute training session on a new machine, process, or compliance issue, consider introducing it with a short video instead of a document. The video should thank your employees for their attendance, explain that they should come to you with any questions on the material, and delve into both the information and why it's important.

Effective communication includes informing your employees that they can access the training material when and how it's most convenient for them. Make sure your content is accessible via mobile and that employees can (if they choose) receive important messages via text or live chat. You can also communicate via social media, depending on your business. At the end of the day, your focus should be on delivering communication in a way that is convenient and customized, ensuring that employees' experiences with your material is as smooth and pleasant as possible.

If electronic communication isn't feasible for your business, that doesn't mean you can throw in the towel. If you have to use paper, ensure your logo is visible and in color. Don't communicate important messages in a way that feels cheap or hurried. Call to mind the example of the poorly communicated benefits increase. What could the founder of WR Manufacturing have done better? To communicate such a significant increase in benefits for his 300 employees, he had booklets printed that were black and white and sixteen pages for about forty cents each. That's $120 to communicate a million-dollar-plus-per-month investment increase—definitely not enough. Instead, his HR staff could have created (with their vendors' involvement) custom training on the new benefits, how to use them effectively, and how much better they were. Links to "Understanding Your New Benefits" videos could have been texted to every eligible employee. Each part of the benefits, from the debit cards to dental, could have had a video made by HR, explaining why they chose that option and what it means for the employees.

SHOW THEM SOME LOVE

Whether electronic or on paper, every cultural communication must include contact points and direct employees where to go for more information. When automating a process, many make the mistake of viewing it only as a push relationship. Obviously, it's important to record employees' acknowledgment or acceptance of information, but part of the process of delivering information is to affect change. In that vein, design a thoughtful approach to how employees will contact you with questions and invite them to do so, whether your company is a five-person crew or a 2,000-strong, multilocation behemoth.

If you put time and effort into providing employees with an open communication channel to HR that mirrors how you communicate, you've established a highly efficient two-way street to help the company make lasting changes. The communication system should effectively collect and store data electronically, "talk" to reporting systems, and distribute information. As with all HR systems, be sure the system not only stores required information but stores it in a way that is searchable.

BROAD, SCALABLE, AND ENTERTAINING

If you make your communication effective, scalable, and entertaining, employees will appreciate the message and take it to heart. Hand out a two-page memo with forty bullet points to cover the same information, though, and they're far less likely to retain your message. This shift moves the needle in how your team responds to change. If you take the time up front to strategically design systems and communications, you won't have to wade through the mire of reaching out to each employee individually down the line. You'll decrease questions and labor associated with follow-up and instead will be able to focus on your people.

A broad, scalable system allows you to rapidly communicate other issues as well—and in a format that is easily accessible at later dates. For example, if an employee needs to look at the details of her benefits plan months after onboarding or refresh her memory about how to request time off, she should be able to access that information electronically. That keeps the repetitive stuff off your desk so you can keep your focus on what matters—your people.

COMMUNICATING COMPANY CULTURE

A built-in bonus of employee life-cycle events is their opportunity to convey a company's culture. Let's explore how communication can help.

Right from the start, onboarding cultural communication should be about more than simply getting paperwork done. During the onboarding process, welcome employees to your company with videos explaining what you do and why. Be sure to include messages from some of your company's key players. Introduce yourself and your HR team, and let your new hires know you're their advocate inside the organization.

In addition, discuss the benefits of working for your organization. Take the time to introduce them to the company culture and tell them what makes your organization great. You can also address broad company structure so they feel more comfortable as they walk the halls the first day. Explain what their department does in comparison to other departments and cover how different departments interact within the company.

THE ANNUAL REVIEW AND YOU

Cultural communication also comes into play during the annual review process. Use clear communication to convey the company's performance and strategy—and, more importantly, how each employee fits into both. Oftentimes, it takes years for individual employees to get a strong sense of place within an organization, but you can accelerate that integration if you're transparent and open.

If there will be changes in benefits, compensation, or PTO, tie that into cultural communication and messaging as well. Resist the urge to hide behind jargon, instead taking a more human and humble approach to conveying company-wide information. Investing in the communication of benefits changes, as we've seen, is particularly important to an honest and positive employer-employee relationship. Even if it's bad news, employees won't feel blindsided by information when it is delivered intelligently with clear explanation.

SHOW YOU CARE

Ad hoc changes are another great opportunity to communicate company culture and engage with employees. If an employee adds a spouse to insurance, gets married, needs maternity leave, or adds a child, those are openings for your company to let them know you value their family and their contribution as part of the culture. In addition, try to make those changes less stressful by making action steps around ad hoc events clear and easy to find.

OFFBOARDING WITH A FOCUS ON COMMUNICATION

During offboarding, the best practice is to focus on the *why* of your company in designing your processes, regardless of whether you're terminating someone, downsizing, or if an employee is quitting. In every offboarding situation, think about the tone and the information you've given them up until that point and try to maintain that level of integrity, openness, and humanity. If, long ago, you spent time welcoming your ex-employee to the organization, don't revert to a feeling of black-and-white memos in a dark room with a lawyer in the corner during offboarding. Doing so would betray your true culture at the worst time, and your remaining employees will see that as the "true" face of your organization.

GO DEEPER

Every company is different, but there are a few best practices to remember as you approach cultural communication for your organization. To learn more, visit **PeopleProcesses.com**, click **Resources**, and download **Five Tips to Improve Cultural Communication in Your Organization.**

PART THREE

———

ROADMAP FOR THE
FIRST 100 DAYS

STEP ONE

DATA GATHERING

If you're ready to automate your HR systems to improve your employee experience, there are tools that can help. This chapter will provide you with a roadmap to use those tools so you can better read the lay of the land on your way to improving your current systems. In the following chapters, I will teach you how to do just that.

For a moment, recall Christy from our introduction. She arrived on the scene at a nonprofit organization focused on helping children with developmental disabilities. The company's mission was noble, but their policies and systems were stymieing their efforts, not enhancing them. With the help of automation, she revitalized the company.

Christy walked into the role with no baggage and a clean slate on which to design system changes. In contrast, if someone charged with improving HR had been there for ten years and suddenly attempted to overhaul the organization, it likely would have had a different set of problems. On one hand, that experienced person knows the unique and troublesome parts of their organization; on the other, that person probably enabled a lot of those stickier processes. The key to success in both situations, though, is having the confidence, vision, and powerful communication ability necessary to make positive, innovative change.

SET THE STAGE FOR SUCCESS

The first step, whether you're a newbie to the organization or it's your second home, is to record all the details about the current state of HR within the company. You know things need to change, and you're confident that with the proper system in place, you can help move new employees rapidly from doe-eyed babes in the woods to efficient and motivated employees who can contribute.

So let's get started on your first 100 days.

The key to getting where you want to go is to first understand where you are—a process that starts with data gathering. The goal of data gathering is to understand and document all the interactions your company has with its most important investments: its employees. Similar to onboarding steps for new clients, you need the same level of detail on paper to figure out where to start.

When I begin this step with my clients, I often receive pushback. Most HR teams are already strapped for time. That is, after all, why they've come to Poplar Financial in the first place. Why, they wonder, should they take *more* time to write everything down? I understand this feeling, but I'm adamant: the first step in fixing your HR systems is to write down how they look today in a comprehensive manner.

It may take two to four days to complete this task, but it's worth it. If your first instinct is to refuse and say the task is too huge, that's proof alone that you *must* do it. If it's hard to put your processes to paper, that just means your processes are in desperate need of work! Just like any goal, reaching the end zone starts with an assessment of your current actions, and documenting them influences your behavior moving forward. Throughout the data-gathering process, you'll gain a strong understanding of what needs to be fixed because you have no choice. Your attention is drawn directly to it.

DATA GATHERING MADE EASY

Find paper and a pen and write down (or for the love of god use a word processor) the four life-cycle events: onboarding, offboarding, annual reviews/open enrollment, and ad hoc. Start with the employee's experience, and think of the steps they go through for each event. Then list how each process looks from HR's perspective. As you work, take care to incorporate enough detail so, in theory, you could hand your file over to someone new (either employee or HR), and they could follow the steps clearly.

Work through the process in small bites. For example, break down annual enrollment or annual review into two parts: one part should be benefits renewal, and the other part should be performance appraisals, bonuses, and pay raises. Then break pay raises, bonuses, and performance appraisals down. Then break appraisals down into selecting metrics, gathering information, and evaluating the information. What do the processes look like for determining employee performance? How do you communicate them? How do you gather your data? What is the time frame for all of those elements?

Don't forget ad hoc events; the promotions, demotions, family status changes, leaves and sabbaticals, and more. Hopefully each of these ad hoc events will only be four or five sentences, but they need to be in there! What are the steps when someone requests extended time off? Even if the current procedure is simply for an employee to ask for their supervisor's okay and nothing else happens, that's fine. Get it on paper.

It's important not to worry about improving processes at this juncture. Simply record them as they are. If you realize you don't have a step for a particular event—offboarding an employee who leaves on bad terms, for example—that's okay. Leave it blank and move on.

Most likely, nothing will be starker than writing down your current processes. On the other end of the spectrum, yours might be a unicorn company that, through the extreme work of yourself and your amazing HR staff, has already improved many of the HR processes that we've discussed thus far. That's wonderful! Stay with me, as the real magic happens when the transformations begin in the next chapter!

Once complete, take a minute to examine your list—again, written from both an employee and an HR perspective. Odds are, you'll find notable differences and opportunities for improvement. These will be your starting points as we move into a closer examination of each component.

GETTING MORE SPECIFIC

Now that you've written down the steps in each life cycle, it's time to move into data gathering for each component. Some components might not necessarily have everyday workflows associated with them, but we should still zoom in for a close evaluation.

BENEFITS AND COMPENSATION

Identify the details of how your compensation is defined and distributed. Ask yourself the following to get started:

- How do you train employees, managers, and HR staff on benefits?
- Do you have an existing method of benchmarking benefits and compensation?
- How do you communicate benefit changes?
- Does your benefit system interact with other events?
- How do your employees enroll in or decline benefits?
- How do your employees request benefits changes?
- If an employee asks for a raise, what is the process for handling that request?
- If a manager needs to cut staff or expenses, do you have a process for communicating that information?
- Once an employee has enrolled in benefits, how does the information move from there to payroll?
- After someone's pay rate has changed in your systems, how does that information reach payroll?

TIMEKEEPING AND ACCRUALS

Identify the details of how you currently tackle timekeeping and accruals. Ask yourself the following to get started:

- How do you train employees, managers, and HR staff on timekeeping and accruals?

- How do your employees interact with timekeeping on a daily basis?
- What do your employees do when they make a mistake in timekeeping or forget to clock in or out?
- How do your employees prove their hours are correct?
- How do supervisors review timekeeping? How do they make corrections and mark their approval?
- From an HR perspective, how do you review employee hours currently in the system?
- How does that information get out of timekeeping and into payroll?
- How are accruals tracked back to the employee level?
- How do your employees request time off and review how much time off they have available?
- Do supervisors have an avenue to see what other people have requested time off so they can balance their schedule?
- How do time off requests get transferred into payroll and tracked in the long term for reporting?
- How do you look at labor costs over time?

SCHEDULING

Identify the details of how your organization approaches scheduling. Ask yourself the following to get started:

- How do you train employees, managers, and HR staff on scheduling?

- How do your employees see their schedule and request changes?
- If allowed, what is your current process for trading shifts?
- Do supervisors have a method to design or communicate the schedule to employees?
- How do supervisors approve changes to the schedule and keep track of who is allowed to work certain shifts?
- Is there a way to keep track of what skills employees have when it's necessary to fill certain shifts?
- What happens when an employee doesn't clock in or fails to come to work?
- What does the supervisor do when they have to fill a shift in an emergency?
- From HR's perspective, how is the schedule balanced in terms of labor costs you've allocated or budgeted?
- How do you get information about schedules in order to help you make decisions about promotions and overall company strategy?
- Does the information from the schedule translate to when people clock in and out?
- How do you tell if people are tardy?
- Is there a system by which people are paid more or less for being late or early, and how does that information get to payroll?

PAYROLL

Identify the details of how your organization approaches payroll. Ask yourself the following to get started:

- How do you train employees, managers, and HR staff on payroll?
- How do your employees receive their pay and update withholding information for tax calculations?
- How do your employees inform you when their address changes?
- How do employees request or receive documentation of their pay for when they apply for a loan or need proof of income?
- What do supervisors do if an employee believes they have a pay discrepancy?
- From an HR perspective, how do you update employee demographic information, such as address and withholding information?
- How are an employee's deductions changed based on information from benefits?
- How do you handle a wage garnishment?
- How do you distribute the actual pay, and what is the process of moving the money from the system into the employee's hands or back again?
- How are hours entered?
- Once you've collected the necessary information and need to run payroll, what is the process for doing so?

- What are the physical steps you take to track hours and determine gross pay?
- How do taxes get paid?
- How are insurance payments made to your vendors?
- How do you compare your insurance bills to your deductions to verify that you are deducting the correct amount?
- How is information reported in your accounting system?
- How does tax information and pay per department flow from payroll into accounting?

REPORTING

Identify the details of how your organization approaches reporting—a component in which your employees likely will not be involved. Ask yourself the following to get started:

- How do you train employees, managers, and HR staff on reporting?
- Do supervisors have access to your reporting system? If so, what information can they access and how do they do it?
- From HR's perspective, how do you provide proof that your timekeeping/benefits/training systems are in compliance?
- When it comes to benefits, how do you prove employees authorized deductions or benefits?

- How do you prove your employees were offered benefits but declined them?
- How do you prove you complied with COBRA?
- How do you prove the time and date a particular employee worked and that the shift was approved by a manager?
- What is the process to double-check if an employee was paid overtime or minimum wage in compliance with the law?
- For onboarding, where do you store and access employee documents, and how would you produce this information if someone were to request it?
- How do you store and report training data?
- Can you generate broad strategic information like trends, cost over time, overtime information, and tardy information across the whole organization? How do you turn this information into usable reports?

COMPLIANCE

Identify the details of how your organization approaches compliance. Ask yourself the following to get started:

- How do you train employees, managers, and HR staff on compliance?
- Do you have a solid process to stay updated on upcoming changes in compliance that will affect your organization?

- What is your method for communicating changes or getting additional signed paperwork?
- Is there a process for auditing current systems for compliance?
- What do you do when you come across a compliance situation you are unsure how to handle?
- Do you know how to verify if each of your underlying components is compliant?

CULTURAL COMMUNICATIONS

Identify the details of how your organization approaches cultural communication. Ask yourself the following to get started:

- How do you train employees, managers, and HR staff on cultural communications?
- How does your organization communicate the structure of the organization, the employee's role in the organization, and the strategic vision of the corporation?
- Does HR have a standard method to distribute information?
- How is the employee informed of financial changes that would affect them, whether that includes pay raises, promotions, or changes in benefits costs?
- When you make communications, do you have to generate them from scratch, or do you have templates at the ready?

- If you have communication templates, where do you store them, how do you access them, and how do you distribute them?
- How do you communicate department-specific information?
- How do you communicate company-wide information?
- Do you have a system that allows you to call-blast a recorded message, or do you call everybody individually?
- If your organization has a text messaging system, how are employees grouped, and how is a group text sent?

COMPILE AND CONQUER

Now that you've completed a substantial amount of data gathering, it's time to merge it all into one file on your computer (or print each page and make a paper binder, if you must). Do whatever you need to get your head around all the components and processes in an easily accessible place. If yours is a small company and you don't have many processes, you'll have a small file with only a handful of documents, and that's okay. Maybe you've just been figuring out the answers to the above questions as you've gone along, and there are no processes in place. That's okay. Now is the time to improve!

If you've persevered through this tedious process, recorded

all your information, and compiled that information in one place, you're 80 percent of the way to streamlining HR systems. At the end of the 100 days, you'll have a system in place that will dramatically improve your company's success.

GO DEEPER

To get started, you can download our template document for your current process documents. It has the life cycles and components broken out, along with the sample questions above already included! It's even a Word file, so it's easy for you to edit and add your own processes. Visit **PeopleProcesses.com** and **download** our **People Processes Template**.

STEP TWO

GOAL SETTING

The second step in the roadmap to change is one rooted in imagination. In this step, your HR team and company executives will learn what is missing from your current processes. Then, you can identify what is needed to fill those gaps, together, just like Christy did.

As the newly appointed executive director, Christy found herself in charge of ensuring her organization continued to run as she took time to dig in and learn how processes were handled—a true feat. Before digging in, she gathered key people in a room and asked targeted questions to find the absolutely essential processes that could not be interrupted (we need to keep receiving shipments, we need to keep paying our employees, we need to keep the lights on, etc.). In the next sections, you'll find some of our pivotal strategies you can use in your organization once you're ready to dig in.

IDENTIFY GAPS

As you reviewed and recorded information to the questions posed in the data gathering phase, surely you noticed gaps. Now, take a look at each gap, and jot a note in the margin of the page or in your computer records about what you *don't* see. Don't worry about being too specific; instead, identify any missteps or hurdles that stand out.

LIFE CYCLE ASSESSMENT

Next, it's time to take a deep dive and assess each life cycle, the goal of the event, and the employee experience at different stages. Note these are not comprehensive lists of what the goals should be, but your list will include most of these elements. For example, you may have a goal at open enrollment to increase the number of people who participate in retirement plans or to have the employees more appreciate the benefits provided to them. Feel free to modify the suggestions below to make them more specific to your organization.

ONBOARDING

Your basic goal in onboarding is likely to get paperwork filled out. You want to get your new employee up and running as quickly as possible so they can be a productive member of the team. During the onboarding process, you also want to instill a sense of the company's culture so new team members know what to expect. Overall, your goal is to optimize the employee experience in such a way that it is repeatable, scalable, and effective.

ANNUAL REVIEW AND OPEN ENROLLMENT

One goal of the annual review process, naturally, is to complete necessary paperwork to renew benefits and help employees appreciate and understand the benefits. You also want employees to understand their performance in relation to the company's performance, as well as the vision or goals for both. For example, what are the goals of the employee's department *and* entire company over the next year? Identifying the goal of the life-cycle events here will help you figure out what information to gather and share!

AD HOC EVENTS

The goal for each interaction around an ad hoc event should be to improve morale and boost loyalty. Right now, the goal is to "just get it done." Instead, view each ad hoc event as an opportunity to benefit the employee and the company, and aim to ensure that each event is handled in such a way that it is effective, scalable, and compliant.

OFFBOARDING

A key goal in offboarding is to part ways with an employee

and avoid being sued in the process—a task that generally requires signatures. You also want to strive to minimize the morale disruption of your remaining employees and any effect the departure will have on client-facing operations.

COMPARE YOUR GOALS TO REAL LIFE IN ACTION

With a close look at life-cycle events in hand, now it's time to compare your goals to what you've learned so far. Compare your binder of data to your list of goals. Do your processes support your goals? If your current onboarding process only involves having a new hire sign papers and little else, does that accomplish your goals of introducing them to company culture and instilling a sense of care? If your current offboarding process involves ambushing an employee in a room, having them sign papers, and escorting them off the premises with armed security guards, does that accomplish your goal of maintaining morale for existing employees? The answer is no, but don't fret. You've just identified gaps!

PLUG THE GAPS

Now that you've taken a hard look at your processes and seen your goals, ask yourself what you need to do to fill those gaps and move forward confidently. Take care not to consider constraints or cost yet. Instead, imagine a perfect world where your wish list of all things good in your company could be magically transmitted to the brains of employees, at no cost. What would that system look like? Think about scalability, effectiveness, and compliance. Think about accomplishing your specific goals and what that would look like. Again, write it all down.

For every gap you identify, ask yourself what a modern company—like the ones I've described at length in this book—would do to improve the process. What technology would they leverage, and how would that investment ultimately benefit the organization? What would they need the specific HR component to be able to do in order for the life-cycle event to accomplish its goal? Once you have a vision for what specific components you can improve in your organization, you have the ability to start making changes.

GO DEEPER

For more examples of goals by system and life cycle, visit **PeopleProcesses.com**, click **Resources**, and download our **Sample Goals by Component Guide**.

STEP THREE

NEW SYSTEMS IDENTIFICATION

In the third step on your journey, you'll consider the specifics of new systems that will help you meet your defined goals. In Christy's case, she knew what path she wanted her organization to follow, but she also knew she wasn't a technical expert. She didn't understand the programming behind payroll or other systems, but the good news is she didn't have to. Instead, Christy knew she simply needed to identify the flaws in her current components and ask applicable personnel for details and assistance moving forward. The same goes for you.

IDENTIFY THE PRESENT AND PLAN FOR THE FUTURE

Once you understand what your organization is missing when it comes to your HR processes and have identified your goals around improving them, examine the current status of your systems. What systems does your organization currently outsource, and what have you developed in-house? As you move through this process, continue to identify gaps and pinpoint systems that need replacing or updating. Perhaps you have a payroll system that consists of desktop software that doesn't connect anywhere with other systems—a clear opportunity for improvement.

When you've identified the people processes you need to replace or update, compose a single document describing your ideal system. Utilize your goals for life-cycle events and what you've learned about components, as discussed in earlier chapters. If you are revising your payroll system, you'll need a system that integrates timekeeping and doesn't require much data entry for accruals and scheduling. The system should also automate payment, handle reconciliation of your taxes and insurance payments, and tie into benefits and compensation to automatically update deductions (including supplemental insurances). In addition, that same system should automate garnishment tracking and have a reporting component you can leverage to make strategic decisions.

Take your time and be as specific as you can when developing your plan for what your system needs to include. Outline what needs to be automated, how your employees and HR team will access it, and what methods supervisors will use to ensure it runs smoothly.

Essentially in this step, you're creating a usable request for proposal (RFP) for a systems vendor. You'll send your RFP to potential payroll and HR companies, attorneys, or benefits brokers as a benchmark for your requirements. The RFP will outline what you need done through an outside vendor and will also note what you have the ability to accomplish in-house.

YOUR RFP TOOLBOX

Your end goal of sending an RFP—similar to an HR wish list—is to gather actionable replies from vendors with concrete details of what they can do for you. This process can be exciting, but take care to consider what comes after you make your decision. How much support will you need? How flexible and scalable are the options presented? Asking these important questions before choosing a solution or vendor will help you take the long view and help you ultimately reach your organizational goals.

IT'S ALL IN THE DETAILS

Be detailed in your request. If you want the ability to send employees text messages, for example, don't omit that from your RFP because you think it's too basic or because you think it would be too expensive. Nothing is too basic for your RFP, as it all ties together in the end. If you want your employees to appreciate and understand their benefits through a scalable and compliant system, for example, the ability to text can help communicate important information. And who knows, maybe you will find a vendor (like Poplar Financial) that includes that capability for free.

Plan to take extra time as you add details to your document. You're likely not going to compile component system RFPs all in one day. That's why this is a 100-day roadmap!

MAKE A VENDOR SHOPPING LIST

Make a point to evaluate at least three vendors: my preference is for a local vendor, a national vendor, and someone in-between. Ask for referrals from your friends and coworkers as well.

Even if you've done well on your RFP, vendors will still have questions, and that's a good thing. Give them the chance to interface with you and truly understand what you need. At the end of the day, you're streamlining your HR systems, but you're also establishing a partnership. Be sure to choose a company that is reputable, well established, and that you like working with.

Besides new vendors, it's important to give your current providers a chance to respond to your RFP. If you have a small payroll company doing some of your work, you don't necessarily have to leave them. If your current system is antiquated, perhaps they could suggest a better fit after reviewing your RFP. Existing providers always have an advantage because they know you and your organization—a benefit when it comes to minimizing disruption. If you can improve your HR systems by simply upgrading, unlocking new components, or integrating other vendors into your current system, it will make the switch that much more efficient. Just make sure your current provider has the scale and expertise to handle the whole thing, as switching again in a year would be a pain.

Depending on the size of your organization, some RFPs may be internal. If your organization is small, maybe you simply need a new electronic storage system or a way to connect employees with their payroll information—some of which can be done in-house if you have the appropriate staff.

Whether internal or external, your RFP is critical to making your future investment work for you. Once you've vetted and selected the teams and technologies that will best help you reach your HR goals, it's time to start building out those systems. In the next chapter, I'll explain how.

GO DEEPER

If you feel comfortable, you can contact us directly and share your goals and current processes. From there, Poplar Financial can put together both an RFP and a proposal of our own! If you decide not to go with us, the RFP will allow you to shop around and find someone who fits your organization better. Visit **PeopleProcesses.com** and click **Start a Conversation.**

STEP FOUR

SYSTEMS AND COMMUNICATIONS
BUILD-OUT

The fourth step in your roadmap is an exciting one! Here, you'll begin to build your new system, just like Christy did. She selected new vendors to replace her company's payroll, timekeeping, compliance, and benefits systems. With a full understanding of existing systems, goals, and components required to achieve those goals, Christy set off to develop the systems that would revolutionize her organization—and you can too.

ACTION ITEMS FOR SYSTEM CONSTRUCTION

Before you approach your system build-out, make a time-line of what you want to accomplish with your vendors in the next thirty, sixty, and ninety days. Don't skip this step! As you create your timeline, consider that your vendors will likely have their own ideas of what this schedule should look like, so stay alert. If a vendor claims they can change your payroll system next week, that's not reasonable. While they might be able to have the system in place by then, there's no way it will be adequately communicated to your employees. Ensuring timelines and priorities are in order at the start of a project will save headaches later.

If you're a small business owner, keep in mind that if you have no dedicated HR staff, it may be you scheduling and completing these integrations—a factor that can also affect timelines. Either way, when evaluating your calendar for optimal systems rollout, first replace the systems you already have. If you have an existing payroll system you plan to upgrade, do that first. If you plan to change how employee benefits are communicated, change that piece first. The general rule is simple: do not try to introduce systems you don't have until you've replaced the ones you do.

Another thought is to try and find someone who can do it all. This keeps you from hearing from your benefits broker that the problem is in your payroll system, or your timekeeping provider saying that the onboarding system isn't communicating correctly. While it's nice to think "one-stop shop," I prefer the term "one throat to choke." If something goes wrong, with a singular provider, they can't blame anyone else, and you only have one vendor to beat up until they get it done. Of course, that means that vendor has to be really good!

MAKE THE DATA TRANSFER

The next step in your journey is to transfer all the data from your existing employee systems, whether that means ten years of paperwork stuffed into file folders, an older online or desktop system, or a combination of the two. Some vendors will include that in their pricing, and sometimes it's up to you to input the data. Some vendors will charge a big setup fee for data transfer, which is reasonable. Others, instead, may charge less yet require a longer time commitment, meaning you must commit to staying with that same vendor for a period of time—sometimes years.

At our company, we take the data you have, in whatever form you have, even if that means (as a recent company had) over six-thousand pages of PDF reports. If that is what you have, work with a vendor that will use that. Don't underestimate the value of having all that data converted by an expert team versus you or your team having to both learn the system and input the data!

BUILD COMMUNICATION AROUND THE SYSTEM

Whenever you are tackling your HR systems, overhauling internally, or using an outside source, remember to prioritize communications around your new systems and allow sufficient time to explain and provide training on the changes. Often, your vendor will take care of data management, conversion of information, the build-out, and tax setup. As a result, you can spend your time finding creative ways to pass on details to your employees. In this way, when rollout day comes, your team is prepared and excited about the changes.

Note that the systems and communication build-out can take a month or more, so be patient. Take time to appreciate your investment and focus on ensuring that your employees realize that value too. Remember, communication is that extra investment that really generates a return!

GET AHEAD OF THE CURVE

As your vendors are creating and implementing systems, you have opportunities to get ahead of the curve internally. If you're waiting on your new timekeeping system, use the downtime to review vendor-provided communications around how employees clock in and out, review time sheets, request time off, keep their schedules, and more. Put your own personal spin on the materials before turning them over to your team, and train them before the new processes are live. Preparation breeds success.

So far, you've gathered data, set goals, created your RFP, chosen a vendor, and scheduled your systems and communication build-out. Get excited! Next up is rollout.

GO DEEPER

For more information on how to optimize your systems and communication build-out, visit **PeopleProcesses.com** and **download** our **Pre-Launch Day Checklist.**

STEP FIVE

ROLLOUT

Rollout day is here! You and your team are likely excited for such positive change to take place after all the systems are in place, as you should be. I'm betting you are expecting a long list of tasks here, but if you did the preparation, rollout day will be a cinch!

On her rollout day, Christy started the day off with a quick meeting to remind everyone that the new HR system (including timekeeping, payroll, benefits, compliance, and training) was going live. She reminded them of new time-keeping procedures, actions they needed to take within the new HR system to sign some documents they were distributing, and where they could locate more in-depth training if needed. Because the team had had training on the changes available for weeks beforehand, they felt prepared. Still, some employees had questions or faced bumps in the road. For example, when Rick in accounting tried to log in to the new system using his date of birth for verification, he was denied access. He called HR, and only then did everyone in the organization learn Rick's birthday had been incorrect in the system—for twenty years! Christy's supervisors discovered a few other similar issues, but they were able to take care of them swiftly by correcting information in the new system.

Overall, for Christy, transforming her organization's HR system was nearly a three-month experience. But as for rollout day, after handling a few hiccups, she spent the rest of her day in meetings with fundraisers, interviewing new staff candidates, and brainstorming with board members. In short, she was able to focus on tasks suited to her ability to run the company and affect change.

If you've followed all the steps up to this point, you, too, can look forward to the start of something great.

ITERATION MATTERS

Engaging the organization with a shiny new system is a solid-gold reward for all the work you've put into the project, but don't forget that rollout week is also the time to go back to the early steps of data gathering and capture the details of the new processes too. Ask yourself what the life-cycle events—onboarding, annual review work, ad hoc duties, and offboarding—look like *now* from both an employee and HR perspective. Pass along these observations to your vendor, as it will be easier for them to correct issues if they understand your processes inside and out. In fact, a reputable and competent vendor will have a process dossier about your company, similar to the one you created at the start of this roadmap. After all, a good vendor must maintain service continuity and deliver everything they promised, which is only accomplishable by good operations (and people) processes on their side too!

YOUR JOB HERE IS DONE—OR IS IT?

Rollout day is about celebrating the removal of rote tasks from your plate, but that doesn't mean you can rest just yet. It's critical to allow time for ongoing maintenance at various intervals. If you are an HR manager, your new job is to go through the roadmap again, make sure your process documents are updated, and evaluate whether they meet your goals! Keep identifying and filling gaps. Keep improving. Your goals will change over time, as they should. The first time you revisit the roadmap may be a bear, as you likely didn't catch all your issues the first time around—and that's okay. As you iterate, you'll continue to improve and move your company forward.

This is the true role of a good HR person. Constant

improvement, in a scalable, process-driven way. Your focus on HR will shift from "getting work done" to actually adding value to your organization's people. What can you do to actually improve the lives of the employees? To help them *love* your company? To go above and beyond? That's why lots of us got into this business—not to do routine paperwork again and again and again!

KEEP AN EYE OUT FOR IMPROVEMENT TRIGGERS

You will undoubtedly face issues when overhauling systems. For example, you may find your timekeeping system only works when everyone is in the same time zone, or you could discover a flaw in your text-messaging system that makes it impossible for employees to opt out of group messages. When problems like these arise, revisit your roadmap, contact your vendor, and build the system out again, careful to correct the issue. New issues like this can feel frustrating, but keep in mind that they are also opportunities for improvement. Making the people processes better, more capable, or less error prone, is the fun part!

ROLLOUT TIPS AND CAVEATS

A successful rollout takes work. Here are some tips and caveats to ensure the process goes as smoothly as possible:

- **Be reasonable with your timeline.** Gathering all

required information and defining and communicating goals will take a great deal of time and focus. Remember to be patient and work strategically. Don't beat yourself up if, as you do this, you find there are tons of things to fix. That's okay! Every step forward will pay huge dividends.

- **Give your systems time to work.** Once you've overhauled your HR systems, give them time to work. Your employees might be jumpy the first few weeks after rollout, as they've likely found themselves in a whole new world. Spend extra time with those who are struggling to acclimate. By automating many of the routine tasks, you free up the time to work with those people one-on-one.

- **Elicit feedback from supervisors and employees.** People are at the heart of HR, so don't forget to ask your people what they think of the changes. Ask how they're adjusting and what they think needs to be improved. Solicit feedback. Then, act on it if you feel it's best for the company.

- **Don't take on too much at once.** Change is the base of progress, but take care not to tackle too much at one time. With an integrated system in place, work on one component at a time to make consistent, manageable improvements. Some endeavors, such as moving from a paper-based system to a modern system, require one big push, but once you're there, the day-to-day falls into place. Other processes—making an onboarding video, interviewing department heads, or changing communication around benefits—will take more time and care.

- **Don't fear pushback.** Embrace pushback; don't fear it. Some employees will always like the old way of doing things better, so it's your job to communicate the value of the new way in a manner that's clear, compassionate, and firm. You may not hear complaints until rollout day or the week after, but preparing for objections ahead of time can turn those negative interactions into opportunities for growth.

- **Don't make exceptions.** Sometimes, high-level executives or tenured employees will consider themselves exempt from new processes they don't like right away. This, in fact, couldn't be farther from the truth. For your systems to work as designed, every person in the company must follow them. No exceptions. If you allow exceptions, you are multiplying your work. For scale, your company will have to have processes in place that take into account both the new way of doing things and those exceptions you make. It can, and will, get out of hand quickly!

After rollout day, your job has changed. As an HR manager or business owner performing HR duties, your role is no longer transactional. No more pushing paper. Instead, every day you come to work, you'll have the opportunity to set new goals, find ways to make systems better for your

HR team and your employees, and leverage your people as your competitive advantage.

CONCLUSION

I've said it before, and I'll say it again: an ounce of prevention is worth a pound of cure. Yes, the processes I've outlined in Part 3 of this book can seem time-consuming and painful, and that's because some of them are. However, if you put the appropriate time and effort into the process, you will face less stress moving forward.

Revolutionizing your HR department may feel overwhelming at first, but think of it as building a house: you can slap up a structure that looks good and will work for a time, but you'll quickly discover leak after leak, issue after issue. As a homeowner, your full-time job turns to addressing the symptoms, not the cause. Don't make that mistake when it comes to transforming your HR systems. Build a strong house, and make it better every day. Don't be so busy mopping up the floors that you can't stop to turn off the water!

USE YOUR ROADMAP

Your people processes should unify life-cycle events and optimize every part of your organization. In this book, I've provided you with a roadmap so you can review your current systems, identify the gaps, and optimize your processes moving forward.

If you're interested in enhancing your people processes but don't feel equipped, seek assistance. Share this book with your payroll company, HR staff, attorneys, and CPA. Ask them if they can help you implement these systems if you simply don't have the time.

If you don't want to go it alone, call Poplar Financial, and we will walk you through the steps you need to ultimately create an RFP. Then, we'll teach you how to evaluate multiple vendors—and we'd love to be one, too! We're in it for the long haul, and we'll compete for your business. Whether you utilize our services or not, your organization deserves robust people processes and the systems that support them. Poplar Financial is here to help, every step of the way.

On a personal note, this whole process is what I do and what I love to do. I am passionate about businesses or organizations making their employees' place of work an amazing place to be.

You can reach out to me directly at rhamy@poplarfinancial.com, or contact my company at PoplarFinancial.com. If you aren't ready to contact us yet, that's fine! Go to PeopleProcesses.com and subscribe to the newsletter and podcast. Get to know us, and maybe one day, my team and I can help you.

Thank you for taking the time to read this book. I know it was a time commitment for you, and even if we never meet or speak, I am honored to have had you spend time with my thoughts. You have taken the first *huge* step to improving your people processes, and I am ecstatic to have been part of that.

Now, go out there and get your work done!

ACKNOWLEDGMENTS

I would like to thank the following business owners and HR admins who have, over the years, pushed Poplar Financial (and me personally) to be better. They have presented great problems, feedback, and longtime loyalty. Thank you!

April S.	Jamie B.	Russ D.
Chad D.	Joe C.	Sarah S.
Chris B.	Joycelyn S.	Scott D.
Cindy O.	Ken C.	Susan M.
Derrick A.	Kristen Y.	Tennile T.
Don A.	Maria G.	Toni M.
Donna V.	Paula H.	Wendy D.
Helena P.	Rebecca T.	Willis Y.
Esther H.		

Finally, I'd like to thank all the employees at Poplar Financial. They go above and beyond every day to help our clients, and I so appreciate their effort, work, and loyalty.

ABOUT THE AUTHOR

 **RHAMY ALEJEAL** and his wife, Elizabeth, are the owners of Poplar Financial, a provider of integrated, automated HR processes. Rhamy and his team work with hundreds of companies across the United States, helping them learn how to stop pushing paper and start prioritizing people. In addition, Rhamy serves on the Federal Reserve's Industry Council on Healthcare, providing insights into employer costs and how they affect businesses in today's marketplace. He holds a bachelor's degree in financial economics and an MBA from the University of Memphis. Find him at PoplarFinancial.com, or listen to his podcast at PeopleProcesses.com.